Fire Diary

Elizabeth Washington

Copyright © 2015 Elizabeth Washington.

All rights reserved. No part of this book may be used or reproduced by any means, graphic, electronic, or mechanical, including photocopying, recording, taping or by any information storage retrieval system without the written permission of the publisher except in the case of brief quotations embodied in critical articles and reviews.

WestBow Press books may be ordered through booksellers or by contacting:

WestBow Press
A Division of Thomas Nelson & Zondervan
1663 Liberty Drive
Bloomington, IN 47403
www.westbowpress.com
1 (866) 928-1240

Because of the dynamic nature of the Internet, any web addresses or links contained in this book may have changed since publication and may no longer be valid. The views expressed in this work are solely those of the author and do not necessarily reflect the views of the publisher, and the publisher hereby disclaims any responsibility for them.

Any people depicted in stock imagery provided by Thinkstock are models, and such images are being used for illustrative purposes only. Certain stock imagery © Thinkstock.

ISBN: 978-1-4908-6501-0 (sc)
ISBN: 978-1-4908-6503-4 (hc)
ISBN: 978-1-4908-6502-7 (e)

Library of Congress Control Number: 2014922984

Printed in the United States of America.

WestBow Press rev. date: 2/11/2015

Contents

Prologue vii

Chapter 1:	Bad Wreck	1
Chapter 2:	House Fire	9
Chapter 3:	Attempted Suicide	14
Chapter 4:	An Opportunity Awaits	20
Chapter 5:	Texas	26
Chapter 6:	Dubai	38
Chapter 7:	Arriving in Baghdad	46
Chapter 8:	Taji, Iraq	54
Chapter 9:	Groundhog Day	66
Chapter 10:	Military/Iraq Updates	73
Chapter 11:	Almost Vacation Time!	81
Chapter 12:	Baghdad/Dubai/Europe	87
Chapter 13:	Ireland	92
Chapter 14:	Switzerland	105
Chapter 15:	Italy	111
Chapter 16:	Back to the Desert	120
Chapter 17:	Have I Lost My Mind?	124
Chapter 18:	A Mortar	129
Chapter 19:	Christmas in Iraq	136
Chapter 20:	Coming Home for Good	140
Chapter 21:	What Does the Future Hold?	148
Chapter 22:	The Birth	155
Chapter 23:	The Visitation	161
Chapter 24:	The Fires of Life	164

Epilogue 171

Prologue
Leaving Baghdad

I GAZE UP AT RANDOM bullet holes on the cream-colored exterior. I wonder how many more there were when the war began. If I were in a US airport right now, I would hear the announcement "Do not leave your luggage unattended at any time." I'm apprehensive at the thought of leaving my baggage here at Baghdad International Airport in a makeshift cement tunnel.

I stand among fifty confused US civilians divided into three single-file lines. We do as we're told and leave our luggage behind. The Iraqis direct us out of the dreary, T-wall tunnel and release the K9s to sniff-search our baggage. They pat down each individual.

A man points at me then gestures to a nearby door where an Iraqi woman sits. The woman wearing a headscarf peers out and waves me over. Although it's typical for a female to conduct physical security checks on another female, this is the first airport where I'm completely out of sight from the men while being searched. I'm nervous about the seclusion from my group. I creep into a stifling, cordoned-off room while everyone else stays outside. Two women pat me down then wave me off with a warm smile.

This is my last time leaving Baghdad International Airport (BIAP). I didn't have to go through all of these extra security steps while passing through two months earlier. This minor inconvenience is only the beginning of a long journey ahead.

I tread over the white-tiled flooring of the expansive yet empty foyer to retrieve my flight ticket to Dubai. The handsome hazel-eyed man at the ticket counter was the same man I had seen several months earlier while arriving in the country. He was the one who handed me my Iraqi visa, and I remember my attempts to avoid eye contact with him. Back then, I was trying not to stare at him. He gave me more than a glance as well.

I walk up to the counter and smile at him shyly.

His eyes meet mine. "You are beautiful," he comments unexpectedly.

"You are too!" I pipe back without thinking.

He hands me my ticket, and I scurry away while debating in my mind whether that was a culturally acceptable response.

I appreciate the flattery at this moment, as I'm going through some difficult challenges in my personal life. My self-esteem is suffering and I have a lot of unknowns to handle in my future. To add insult to injury, I'm recovering from a horrible haircut from my last stay in Dubai.

The flight from Baghdad to the United Arab Emirates wasn't too bad. It wasn't until I caught my flight from Dubai to London that my morning nausea turned into sporadic vomiting and several unanticipated trips to the bathroom. I decide to keep a paper receptacle close by for the remaining trek as I continue westbound to the other side of the globe.

Bittersweet emotions are at a pinnacle as I reflect on my recent adventures. Over just a few short years, I've sustained an intimate encounter with life in ways that make me feel as if a decade has passed. Depression, death, trauma, religion, travel, culture, war, peace, rejection, life, and love—as a young and somewhat naïve woman from small-town USA, I didn't anticipate that I would've become acquainted with topics of such magnitude. I've been challenged from more recent events, yet any pain I feel is a miraculous motivation to my soul.

Chapter 1

Bad Wreck

Eighteen Months Ago

Here on the west coast of the state of Washington, it rains frequently and follows a long cycle of gray, sunless days. Today the sun has broken its cycle of hide-and-seek and dominates the sky. The heat blazes compared to normal, and our crew is outside the firehouse enjoying the sunshine while practicing fire-hose drills. On days like this, we want to soak up all the rays of sunshine we can, because it's uncommon.

At completion of our drills, we shed our heavy bunker jackets to cool off. We climb like monkeys to the top of our shiny, red fire engine to reload the hose while one of the guys retrieves bottled water for the crew. He tosses the bottles up to us, and we sloppily gulp them down. Beads of water escape the sides of our careless mouths and trickle down our sweaty necks.

My partner and I walk into the apparatus bay. I pull my suspenders off my shoulders and allow the heavy fire gear to drop to the cement floor. Fire tones echo through the building, and I freeze to hear the incoming call.

"Engine 1, engine 2, aid 1, aid 2, respond to a motor-vehicle accident on Highway 6," the dispatcher announces.

My bunker pants are down around my ankles, acting as restraints and disabling me from quick movements. I grasp my suspenders and pull them up over my shoulders to release the restraints. Now ambulatory, I hustle over to the rest of my gear.

We jump into our aid unit and drive south with lights flashing and sirens piercing through the previously silent rural neighborhood. The sky is a beautiful, rich blue, and it's hard to think of a happier day for someone to have a potentially unhappy afternoon because of an accident.

While winding along the curvy back roads, the oncoming vehicles peel to their right like dominos, one car after the other, clearing the road and allowing our emergency mission to continue.

The wreck occurred a few miles out of our district, so we know we will arrive just after the fire engine and medic unit. Updates come in quickly over the radio—potentially six patients and something about a bloody, broken nose. Since I live in this district, I'm familiar with the roads and don't need the map to direct my partner to the scene.

We arrive at a two-car, head-on collision on a busy road, accompanied by a fire engine, a medic unit, another aid unit, a battalion unit, and a few law-enforcement vehicles. State patrol officers in their shiny shoes and crisp, dark uniforms control traffic while the fire crews labor away and prepare the heavy-duty extrication tools. All personnel appear calm, lending a façade of organization to the scene. Regardless of the calm appearance, I have an instant sense that this is a more serious accident than previously anticipated.

My partner and I step out of the aid unit, and we're greeted by the chief, who guides my partner to prepare the power unit for the Jaws of Life.

"Lizzy, you have patient care." He directs me assertively as he points to the driver of a small sports car. I swing the large med bag over my shoulder and trudge over to the driver's side of a red car. Already, I break a sweat in my thick bunker gear and black helmet as I walk the short distance.

The vehicle is occupied by two men sitting upright, conscious, and silent, without much movement. The red sports car doesn't have a top, and the sun is beating down on their heads as if taunting them with its happy light. I glance over at the other vehicle involved in the wreck and see an engine and aid crew at work extricating those victims.

I arrive at the side of the car and loom over a middle-aged, bearded man. His legs are trapped by the dashboard of his small, compact convertible. First I notice the thick blood running from under his chin all the way down to his pelvis and coating the front of his shirt in a V shape. Then I notice the broken nose that was mentioned on the radio, only that description was a severe understatement. His nose is literally inverted into his skull, and the bones from under the surrounding tissue are revealed.

It's common to arrive at a scene that's much different from the information given to us. It reminds me of the game of telephone that I played as a kid. In real life, it begins with a hysterical bystander relaying information to the 911 dispatcher. Through the sobbing and screaming, the dispatcher translates the message and provides a description over the radio to the emergency personnel.

The man is pinned behind his dashboard and can't be extricated until the hydraulic tools are available to cut the door off. I evaluate the rest of him at this awkward angle—I am next to the car—when his right arm catches my eye. His elbow is bent and propped on the center console, and his radius and ulna are broken in half with skin still intact. The arm is flopped over with hand hanging downward, unusable.

My old partner, Cookie, is talking to the passenger on the other side, who is also trapped. Cookie looks up at me and senses that I want to help this man, but there's nothing I can do but buy time. I'm usually confident when working with motor-vehicle-accident patients, but I feel a little stunned and worthless right now. I look across the car at Cookie, and it's as if he reads my mind and knows what to say.

"Lizzy, just talk to him."

I appreciate Cookie's calm and reassuring tone right now. I ask the man some questions to assess his level of consciousness.

"I can't feel my legs," the man says.

Of all the things I see for him to complain about, I wouldn't have thought of his legs.

I lean over him to see the other side of his face. His right eye is missing and I can see through the empty hole into his broken, blood-red skull. I've seen trauma before, but this is different. This man sits silently, alert, and able to communicate, while having sustained wretched injuries that would typically send someone into writhing, cathartic outbursts.

The man turns his head so that he can see his right arm, which is broken in half. He hadn't noticed the arm previously because it's adjacent to his missing eye. He responds to this sight by taking his good left hand and batting at his floppy right hand, making it sway back and forth. I redirect his view forward and try to comfort him, although this man isn't complaining, crying, or even cringing. He's in such shock to his condition that he remains emotionless.

Chief delegates everyone to their next duties based on his strategic oversight. I help to extricate Cookie's patient from the passenger seat. We stand up on the car behind the patient and pull him up out of the car onto a backboard. Chief assigns me to patient care for this young man after he's freed from the vehicle.

We anticipate the arrival of additional medic units to the scene and have Life Flight en route for my first patient.

Now I provide care to my new patient while he lies on the road on a backboard because there isn't an extra aid unit available. I kneel beside the young man while taking his blood pressure and checking his vital signs. A patient in his condition usually has at least two people, if not three, giving care—one to ask questions and do paperwork, one to clean and bandage wounds, and one to take vitals. This man seems to have some internal bleeding and needs advanced care. Our personnel are spread thin, and I'm just doing the best I can to help him until the next paramedic unit arrives.

The heat is intense with all my gear on, and I start to drip beads of sweat from my forehead down to the tip of my nose. The last thing this guy needs is for me to drip sweat on him.

I try to shield his face from the sun, but it's difficult to do while cleaning and dressing the large laceration on his knee. His knee was sliced and filleted open into a football shape about six inches long and six inches wide and is coated in glass fragments. I'm able to provide basic care for him and document his information before transferring care to the paramedics who arrive.

I'm next directed to help pull out the passengers of the other vehicle. We extricate a woman and her daughter and transport the daughter to the nearby hospital while another crew transports her mother.

Luckily, this girl doesn't seem to have been physically affected by the accident. In fact, she has no complaints and seems quite oblivious to the extreme circumstances surrounding her.

After noting her condition and vitals, she and I talk for a bit. The young girl is in junior high and excited that she just celebrated a birthday with her family. They went to a concert and saw one of the latest popular boy bands. I'm charmed by her sweet disposition, and for a moment, I'm oblivious to the looming aftermath of a horrific accident.

We arrive at the hospital, and I see my fellow firefighters from the other transport unit. They're in their T-shirts with their bunker pants still on, suspenders hanging down by their sides. They stand next to an empty gurney. Once they make eye contact, they gesture to me.

I can tell they don't want my patient to hear what they're saying. I scrunch my eyebrows at them as if it will help me to hear them better. "What?"

"Don't tell her that her mom has died," one whispers.

The chills come over me as I awkwardly roll the girl by on the gurney, trying not to stammer or change the previous tone of our lighthearted conversation. The blood drains from my face as I recall pulling her mother from the passenger seat. I hadn't realized the extent of her condition as we freed her unconscious body from the metal wreckage.

After transferring care to the emergency room nurses, I overhear the doctor speaking to the girl as he delivers the heavy news. I see her through the curtains, and she nods in understanding. It looks like she doesn't believe what she's hearing. I rush away to finish my paperwork. Actually, I rush away because I don't want to see her true emotions come through when the girl finally grasps onto the reality that she no longer has a mother.

It's been a hard day for everyone and I'm surprised by the mother's death. While sitting in the passenger seat, as we return to the station, a rush of anger overcomes me. It's one of those overpowering emotions where you feel as if you have no outlet and you just want to scream. Simultaneously, I don't want to lose my cool in front of my partner, so I'm internalizing it all. This isn't a common emotion for me; I don't understand the meaning of my reaction.

Back at the station, we congregate in the apparatus bay to finish the lengthy cleanup and restocking process. Disinfecting and replenishing our depleted medical supplies is a necessity.

There are several of us cleaning up at the firehouse, personnel representing three different fire stations. I spot a gurney with a yellow blanket covering a body. It's the body of my first patient, the man with the broken nose. Sometimes, we have to bring bodies back to the station for the coroner to come pick up.

I walk over to him and see his lower legs and feet hanging out. A medic walks to my side to accompany me.

I lift the yellow blanket with my blue-gloved hand. "When did he die?"

The medic also takes a blue-gloved hand and holds up part of the blanket. "As soon as they pulled him out. The car was probably holding him together. Releasing him from that trap allowed internal bleeding to occur at a rapid rate." The medic notices my curiosity and allows me to view the body.

I'm able to see the lower part of his body that was pinned beneath the dashboard. The tibia of his left leg is broken in half and protruding all the way through his skin. I assess his fatal wounds curiously and respectfully. The previous environment was loud, hot, and busy, and now I examine him in a quiet, calm atmosphere. I'm able to reflect and feel calmer.

The last thing I notice before stepping away from the man is a tooth lying by his side on the gurney.

The medic grasps the tooth with his gloved hand. "Oh wow, I didn't even know that was there."

As emergency personnel, we have to be somewhat jaded to the realities of life; otherwise, it would be difficult to stay in this line of work. Banter and pragmatic comments are normal after running calls, but this stands out to me, more than typical. On this occasion, I'm not quite ready to return to my normal duties.

When the rigs are back in service, the fury that I felt earlier subsides completely and my energy drains from all the strong emotions.

I notice a change in my behavior and don't want to be around anyone. I just want to be secluded and alone with my strange feelings. This isn't like me. I've been to a lot of calls and I never have this reaction.

I decide to talk to my partner. I force myself to fess up that I'm in need of a critical incident stress debriefing (CISD). He takes my request seriously and promptly speaks with Chief.

The operations chief and one of the medics join me in an office to discuss the events while resting on leather couches. They confess that there were times when they too have needed someone to talk to after a call. They allow me the opportunity to talk and say whatever I need to, to get out the emotions and discuss the things bothering me from the accident.

"It's okay," they reassure me.

"I remember the first time I needed a CISD," Chief says as he proceeds to tell me his story.

The medic follows up by telling the story of his first difficult call. I can tell it makes them feel better to talk about their stories as well, even though they were years ago.

I feel relieved after talking to them. I just needed to acknowledge my emotions and move on.

The accident occurred close to my home. Every day I see the spray paint on the road, marking the location of the accident, and I'm reminded of that day. About a week after the CISD, while driving past the spray paint, I have a vivid memory of a critical piece that I hadn't acknowledged until now.

My previous sense of peace is destroyed when I remember a gesture that the dying man made toward me. While I stood by his car, he reached out his left hand to me. I remember the blazing sun shining down on his trembling palm as he reached up to me with every bit of strength that he could muster. It was as if he wanted me to hold his hand. I don't recall what exactly went on in my mind at the time, but I may not have held his hand because I didn't want to appear unprofessional. At this thought, I'm instantly heartbroken. Could I have comforted this man in his last moments and neglected to do so? Oh, how tragic! I always pride myself on my level of empathy and nurturing during patient care. I've held people's hands upon their gestured request while riding to the hospital. Why didn't I do this for him? This may be difficult for me to get over.

Chapter 2

House Fire

Ever since I was a young girl, I wanted to be a firefighter. Well, I wanted to be a whole lot of things while growing up. I vividly remember a neighbor kid asking me, "What are you going to be when you grow up?" I replied confidently that I would be a doctor, a singer, a teacher, a pilot, and a fireman. "You can't be all of those," he replied snidely. "You can only be one." I stared at the pavement for a moment, stunned and heartbroken as I processed this new information.

My desire to become a firefighter didn't dissipate. Before I threw on my first set of bunker gear and became a firefighter, I knew very little about the emergency services. I didn't realize that my speculations were way off from the reality. "Fire," as I used to call it, is comprised of a completely different culture on its own. Once you enter this field, you receive insight on the lives of human beings in a way that you may have never seen otherwise.

When I finally had the opportunity to go through recruit school as an adult, I was ecstatic and became passionate about the fire and emergency medical services. I desired the opportunity to help people during their greatest time of need, and I enjoy the challenge to continuously develop my knowledge. I feel this is my calling and the final destination of all my career choices.

Right before dawn, the tones ring through the firehouse. I'm startled as I jump up in a daze. Stumbling out of my bed and feeling sort of cross-eyed, I struggle to put my socks on quickly. I can't sleep well with my socks or my watch on, so it's absolutely routine that I first grab my nicely laid-out socks before heading out of my bedroom door to the apparatus bay. I don't put my watch on because I can tell by the tones that this isn't a medical call. I won't need to use my watch for counting a pulse rate, and I won't be jumping into the aid unit. This is a structure fire.

It's a second alarm fire and we're needed as mutual aid for the department down the road. The radio traffic informs us that we're needed for manpower, tools, and water. My partner jumps in the engine while I take the water tender with one of the resident firefighters.

Fire hydrants are few and far between in the country, so we rely on water tenders to provide the fire engine with enough water.

The drive to the nearby fire district is a winding, narrow road. It's difficult to drive quickly in the water tender with 2,500 gallons of water sloshing around. Each corner feels like the top-heavy tank will flip over. The diesel engine rattles. The adrenaline makes my foot shake vigorously in my big rubber boots as I stomp on the accelerator.

I try to keep up with the fire engine, but our tanker doesn't take the turns smoothly. The bright red and white flashing lights from the engine gradually disappear from our view. My opportunity to follow the engine to the scene is gone, so we have to resort to the map book and memory of street names to find where we're going.

A night-light ambiance illuminates the sky from the moon and all the stars. My passenger and I look up for a sign or some sort of direction of the fire. In the distance, we spot a large, black column of smoke growing tall like a silhouette against the starry sky. We now know exactly where we're going.

We arrive on scene to a single-story, wood frame, residential structure with smoke billowing out of the windows. We're directed to take fire attack through the back side of the house. My partner and I don our self-contained breathing apparatus (SCBA) and facemasks.

Our hands and fingers work nimbly through the multiple steps to put on our gear. We've rehearsed this over and over in case of a moment like this. We grab the hose line and proceed to the back door.

The home is blackened from the smoke, impairing a good visual of the inside, but the fire locations are bright and evident in the dark. Flames rip and smoke permeates the confines of the structure. I rest my hand on the bale of the nozzle and prepare to utilize purposeful extinguishment techniques.

The fire is loud, as are the sounds of our every breath. Each inhalation and exhalation is emphasized by the bulky breathing apparatus. With adrenaline coursing through my body, I focus on breathing slowly and calmly to conserve air.

The first doorframe inside the home blazes with fire. I aim the nozzle, open the bale to release the pressurized water, and extinguish the dancing flames. The source of the fire is still unknown, and annihilating the flames on the doorframe doesn't stop the smoke from emerging. The black smoke is indicative of a fire continuing to brew and hide somewhere nearby.

We advance one more step into the house, not knowing that the floor suffers from a lack of structural integrity. With my next step, the weakened floorboards give away beneath me and I crash through to the floor. My right leg dangles into the crawl space below. My left leg and upper body manage to remain above floor level and I'm practically doing the splits right now. The jagged floorboards jab into the back of my upper thigh while I dangle precariously. Heat radiates against my leg from the fire growing under the floor. I collect my thoughts. This is no time to panic! My partner grabs me and yanks me out of the hole. I'm uninjured and thankful for my partner and the protection of my bunker gear. I'm still determined to continue this fight.

We relocate to the kitchen and kneel down on the wood flooring. I feel heat under my knees as I shove the nozzle into a different hole in the floorboards and flood the space below with pressurized water. Soon, we see the signs of a retreating fire. We back out, as the next crew arrives to give us a break.

My partner and I step outside and I feel a rush of excitement from the adrenaline and abstract emotions of recent activity. We remove our facemasks and helmet to take a deep breath of the cool, dewy morning air. Sweat dissipates off our bodies in a white sheen of steam floating from our head and body. It twirls gently as it disappears into the wind. We kneel on the grass for a moment to catch our breath.

"That was fun!" I think, knowing that probably sounds crazy to anyone outside the realm of the fire service.

The fire is out, and the sun is rising. The final crew is inside the home making sure there's no potential for the fire to reignite. We reload the tools that are no longer in use and they are covered in black soot. We will have to clean them when we return to the firehouse.

My captain takes a good look at me and smirks. "It never fails; you always seem to get soot on your face no matter what kind or size of fire."

I laugh at his comment because he points this out to me every time, and he's always right. If we get called out to a tiny brush fire, I'll come home with at least a smudge of black on my cheek or forehead.

The fire investigators are called to the scene. The family living in the home evacuated once they noticed the fire so there were no lives lost. Significant damage is done to the home, but many personal belongings are salvaged.

We don't get many fire calls, but when we do, I'm thankful to have all the protective equipment, a good partner on the line, and all the apparatus necessary to get the job done while keeping our firefighters safe.

At 0730 (7:30 a.m.), one fire crew is off duty while the next crew takes over for the next twenty-four-hour shift. It's a well-earned two days off after running calls all night. For me, sleep deprivation accumulated over weeks of middle-of-the-night calls will lead to strange sleep behavior.

One night, I was on shift and fell fast asleep in my fire station bed. I dreamed the rest of my shift members took the fire engine out of the apparatus bay to wash. While still asleep, I got up out of bed, opened the door, and walked into the hallway toward the apparatus bay. It was about two in the morning when one of the other firefighters passed me in the hallway.

He gives me a suspicious grin. "Lizzy? What are you doing?"

At that moment, I realized I was sleep walking.

"I'm going to use the bathroom," I mumbled to him. I turned around and walked back into my bedroom.

Another time, I fell asleep on a recliner while the rest of my shift was still up watching television. I remember dreaming about singing and blurting out a couple of random notes. I felt a little embarrassed.

Chapter 3
Attempted Suicide

Asleep at the firehouse, in my twin bed, the first sound of the house alarm goes off. Adrenaline pumps through my blood stream and my heart pounds hard in my chest. I leap out of bed, put my socks and digital-watch on, grab my pager, and race out the door. It's a medical call: "attempted suicide."

I put on my bunker pants to hide my pajama bottoms and jump into the aid unit.

The address of the incident is at the farthest end of our district, up in the woods. This is going to be a long drive. The directions aren't clear on our mobile computer dispatch so we don't know exactly how to get there. It's dark and the roads are wet and glistening as our emergency lights flicker across the pavement.

Address markings on these homes have been neglected. The painted numbers have faded and made them camouflage into the exterior walls of the home, making it nearly impossible to distinguish in the dark.

We creep by houses and peer out our windows, unable to find the address. I turn off our flashing lights since there's no traffic and we may just disturb people as they sleep.

We drive one direction and realize that we have to turn the whole box-shaped rig around to see if we missed the house. This happens several times as we pace back and forth in the aid unit. How embarrassing! We radio the dispatcher and ask them to contact the homeowners to provide further directions.

Emergency lights flash in the distance as two cop cars catch up with us. One of the cops pulls into a driveway and shines a light on the front of the house. Nope, that isn't it.

We head up the road and then turn back around. I'm thankful no one else is out on the road to watch us look incapable of our job as we go back and forth.

As we drive by the home that the cop shined a light into, we see a man standing outside. I roll down the window in anticipation that he has information for us.

He puffs out his chest. "What are you doing in my driveway at four in the morning?"

"Sorry, sir. We have an emergency." I proceed to ask if he knows where the mystery address is located.

The man's body language is aggressive like he's preparing for a fight; instead, he throws up his arm and points. "It's way up this dirt road."

"Thank you, sir."

The two cop cars shoot up the road in front of us and we follow behind on a bumpy, muddy, poor excuse of a road.

We arrive to a log-cabin house and I notice a young woman in her midtwenties, with blood all over her arms, shirt, and face. The cops talk to her and her family. They lounge under the illumination of the front-porch light, acting as if nothing major occurred.

I step out of the aid unit in my bunker pants and navy-blue T-shirt. It's chilly outside and I wish I had my sweatshirt with me. I walk up the front-porch steps wearing my blue latex gloves and medical bag over my shoulder. I approach the young woman and proceed with my normal medical questions in order to fill out a report for the hospital.

She's a beautiful girl with dark eyes and long, curly, brown hair. I take her hands gently and rotate them palms up to see the deep self-inflicted wounds on both forearms. The woman is cooperative with me as I bandage her wounds and then guide her into the back of the aid unit to get her out of the cold of the night.

There are three deep, horizontal lacerations on each forearm that have bled a great amount. The bleeding has stopped, which tells me that she did this quite a while ago. I've seen attempted wrist slashings in the past, but this woman seems determined, as her wounds are deep. I cleanse and wrap her wrists then clean the blood from her face. All the while, I talk to her and try to help her feel safe.

As my partner hops in the front seat and drives us to the hospital, I ask the girl why she decided to do this to herself. She tells me she was raped by a guy friend and her husband found out but doesn't believe that it was undesired physical contact. She becomes nauseous. I help her to aim into the plastic barf bag as she vomits up half a bottle's worth of red wine. She sobs and hyperventilates for a moment.

Finally, she's calm and pulls down the bandage on one of her wrists to reveal her wounds. I watch her face as she gazes at her self-inflicted lacerations. While peering down at her bloody wrists, her pupils dilate. The look in her eyes almost appears proud as she stares at the deep, fleshy slice marks.

I talk with her more during the drive and she's grateful of my kindness and lack of judgment. It's a long trip to the hospital and she frequently pulls down the bandages to gaze at her wounds. I wish her the best as we transfer her care to the hospital emergency room.

I have the emotional façade of any emergency personnel during a medical situation: calm, kind, and levelheaded. I'm able to react in a subjective manner to the situation at hand with all emotions aside. Some of the worst things I've seen don't affect me as much as I expected they would, and other things affect me more than I would've guessed. When the call is over, some pieces of the scene are left with me.

I'm secretly intrigued by this woman. Her exterior mutilation reflects her inner turmoil. She probably felt proud because she now has a visible indication of the chaos inside and maybe it gives her a sense of control over her situation, although it doesn't. I didn't tell her, but her wounds were ones I've imagined as my own a time or two. I'm a strong woman; I couldn't ever be so weak to actually do such a thing to myself. She probably has worse problems than me. Doesn't she? Or are our problems only as great as we allow them to be?

There's no going to sleep at the firehouse after that call. At least this was a 4:00 a.m. call and not a 3:00 a.m. call. For some reason, I'm at my worst at 3:00 a.m. and might as well be sleep walking. At 4:00 a.m., I can do well on a call and usually get back to the firehouse in time to finish up paperwork and start a pot of coffee.

I always envied those who could stay on a focused life path. They go to school, get good grades, become married with kids, stay at one job, and live a well-harvested life. I didn't think I could ever be so disciplined to focus on anything for a length of time. I attended four different colleges in the five years that it took me to graduate. During college, I worked five different part-time jobs in three different cities. My behavior wasn't indicative of a person who wanted to settle down anytime soon. I couldn't even figure out if I was ambitious or just lost. I chose to view it as ambition but figured everyone else suspected I was lost.

Regardless, I forced myself to follow what I thought was ideal. At twenty-three years old, in a one-week span, I graduated college, got married, bought my first house, and started a career. I was proud of myself, but it all happened so quickly. Just like a broke man winning the lottery, I didn't have the discipline to handle all the new responsibility at once.

Three short years after I married, it was over. My relationship ended because of my inability to find contentment. Even still, there seems to be no relief to my restless spirit, the desire to find what it is I'm missing in life. Why is there an emptiness that I can't seem to fill? Besides longing for understanding, the grieving from divorce is a terrible experience.

Now I live alone. He and I didn't have babies so it's just me and my dog and cat. On occasion, I rent out a room to help pay the mortgage, but for the most part, I'm alone. I have so much time to myself to go work out, shoot my bow, work on the yard, grab a beer with my buddies, or go shopping at the mall. It's liberating to have free time for myself, but when I'm lonely, it's often too much unstructured time.

The excess time provides opportunity for my mind to linger over the things that bother me with my recent divorce and other relationships which have gone awry as a consequence. In fact, my mind plagues me most every day lately and it takes all the positive energy I can muster to get up each morning.

I'm at a point in life where every morning I need to pray hard for strength and guidance and peace to make it through the day. I just want to hold my head up during this lonely time and remind myself that God has a purpose for my being.

Besides the relentless feeling of emptiness in my heart, I've struggled with depression since I was a teenager.

After many years of emotional struggles, I'm able to grasp some strength in managing my depression through exercise, healthy eating, and basic awareness. Even with my newfound strength, I'm struggling at this juncture in life and challenged to maintain the inward peace I normally can find. For the first time in a long time, I dwindle into a deep and dark depression.

It's nighttime. I'm lying on my twin bed, wide-awake. My thoughts sink deeper and deeper into the dark abyss of emptiness and loneliness. My heart gives up the fight and the worst side of everything possible in life rears its demonic head. The racing thoughts touch on everything from the past and present to my lack of enthusiasm for the future. My mind rests momentarily on the girl who slit her wrists and then I contemplate my own life and death.

Tears linger as heavy drops and adhere to my lower lids. I lie motionless for hours, crippled by thoughts which cause my stillness. They intensify and worsen. I'm consumed by grief, no longer wanting to live.

Suddenly, out of nowhere, I feel a smile cross my face and I'm filled with happiness. I'm still wide-awake, but I'm no longer in my bed; I'm in a vision. My head lands gently into a field of grass with the sun in my eyes. I'm surrounded by tall grass that's been bleached from the warm summer days. The sun is low in the sky and reflects an orange glow upon a child. It's a little girl, maybe two years old, with long, dark hair. The little girl is smiling and I can see the right side of her face with a chubby, little cheek as she smiles. She runs by me, dress flowing in the breeze. I'm filled with joy, and this little girl—she is my daughter.

The vision vanishes as quickly as it appeared and I'm stunned to find myself back in my bed. I stop feeling sorry for myself instantly and wipe my eyes. I have a knowing, deep in my soul, that I just saw a moment of my future. I would say I don't believe it, but it just happened. Something is telling me that I have someone very special to live for.

Chapter 4
An Opportunity Awaits

ALTHOUGH HEALING FROM DIVORCE AND living alone, I find some comfort in achieving a small amount of consistency in one aspect of life. I've established a career and developed roots in my occupation as a career firefighter in the northwest. The daily preparation and occasional fire or EMS call is challenging and rewarding. I've spent too many years moving and changing jobs. I desire to find a place to throw my anchor and call home.

So why is there still a lingering of self-disapproval? It's as if I've grown too comfortable resting on previous achievements and stopped striving for success in other areas. I want to expand my wisdom and perspective on life even more.

My restless spirit is calling and change looms on the horizon. Part of me doesn't want to go anywhere because I'm comfortable. But there's a tug on my heart to do something that will push me out of my comfort zone. The desire comes from somewhere deep, as if I need to seek and find my destiny.

The dust has settled from the struggles in my personal life and I've faced the demons instead of running away. For the first time in my life, I've realized it was better to stay and face the challenges. I feel confident that I'm mentally prepared to move forward and discover a new direction for my life. In fact, I know I need something different. A transition needs to be made and my heart is calling me to make a drastic decision.

My desire is to become a firefighter on a military base, in a war zone. This aspiration is so great that it consumes my thoughts constantly, every day.

I heard about firefighting in Iraq a few years back and was intrigued by the idea. My intrigue has grown into an obsession, and now I can't stop thinking about the opportunity and mentioning it to people. It's been on my mind so much that I talk about it constantly to friends. I don't know when, or if, I will go, but I tell people that I plan to go. My mind has fixated on this path for over a year now and it's all I can think about.

Now that I've been in the fire service for a few years, I'm done talking about going to Iraq. I will do what needs to be done for it to become reality.

I suppose I should start informing my family. My mom, dad, sister, and wonderful stepparents should all know about this future endeavor. I've told my friends, but I'm hesitant to discuss it with those closest to me.

I finally work up the nerve to tell my dad. He's distressed about the proposition and tries to convince me to do otherwise. "Yeah, it's not safe over there. People are still getting killed and injured, even on base. So … yeah, you shouldn't go then." His tone is calm and decisive. I feel bad because I can tell he thinks his personal decision will transfer into my own desire through osmosis.

Whenever I have an opportunity to mention the idea to my sister or mother, I shy away. I don't want them to be scared. I know they will find out through a third party anyway.

I'm such a chicken! So I'm willing to go into burning buildings, and I'm willing to enter a war zone as a civilian, but I won't start a simple conversation with my family? I sit back and realize how silly this sounds.

My friend Matt is currently working in Tikrit, Iraq, and I've been able to ask him a few questions about the process. I met Matt when he worked for a nearby fire station. I asked him questions about the whole experience but there are really too many unknowns and so many questions that could be asked. It's difficult to imagine what the living situations would be like, and I know that experiences vary from person to person. Matt informs me that the hiring process occurs quickly because they need firefighters in the field to recover for the turnover rate of one-year contracts. I can expect that life will change dramatically once I begin the process.

My friend Kathye was a firefighter in Iraq as well and it's been wonderful to have another woman's perspective on the experience. She said it gets irritating at times because you will get stares everywhere you go on base since the male-female ratio drastically differs from in the States. She was the only female firefighter on her base. The percentage of women in the fire service is small, but growing. The percentage of us in Iraq is even smaller. I've known Kathye for many years now and I've always found her to be an admirable and hardworking woman.

Only a month after starting the application process, I receive a letter in the mail. My heart begins to race as I see the envelope addressed with my name. I almost don't want to open it! This little envelope contains either the confirmation or dismissal of my greatest ambition.

I hesitate, and then I flip the envelope to expose the adhesive flap. With my heart pounding, I dig my pointer finger into the corner of the envelope and rip the top fold open in a jagged line. As I unfold the paper, the word "congratulations" catches my eye. A big smile spreads across my face. I've received an offer to work as a contract firefighter in Iraq.

Wow! I'm elated! I almost can't believe that I will really be going to the Middle East on such a unique journey.

My family doesn't share the same sentiments at all. They're frightened and upset. As much as they disapprove, they know my spirit and that I'm beyond the point of convincing to do anything other than to go to Iraq.

The purpose of this project is to support the military in their efforts with Operation Iraqi Freedom. When soldiers initially set foot in Iraq and began to house on bases around the country, it was found that there was a need for regular, ongoing fire and safety inspections. The electrical aspects of the structures are not up to the same standards as in the United States and there are documented deaths of soldiers in Iraq due to noncombat-oriented tasks. There were electrocution deaths from showering due to absence of appropriate electrical grounding in containerized housing units (CHU) and a large amount of electrical fires because of the different adapters and voltages.

Along with fire inspections, contract firefighters respond to fire and EMS calls, provide fire safety education to military personnel and third-country nationals (a TCN is someone from a country other than USA or Iraq), and respond to airfield emergencies if there are hard landings or fires associated with aircrafts. It would be an honor to support the military and see firsthand what their lives are like while living in a combat zone.

There's something to say about the feeling of being shipped over to the Middle East within a few short weeks. Now that I'm going through the initial process of going to Iraq, it all seems so surreal. Although I've done research on this position, I really have no idea what I'm getting myself into. I don't know what kind of people I will be around or what kind of roof I will be sleeping under. Will I be camping out? Will people be nice to me? All I really am sure of is that I'm packing lightly and traveling alone into the unknown.

I know that Iraq is at war but has quieted down since the soldiers first arrived several years ago. I know that there have been many deaths and a lot of hostility, but I'm not afraid of being hurt or killed. I'm more afraid of what type of men I will have to work around and how they will treat me. In fact, being around strange men and possibly being the only woman is my biggest fear because I don't know how I will be treated.

Having worked in the fire service for a few years now, I've grown comfortable working and being around men. I'm confident in my abilities and I know that I can learn and do what my peers can do.

Most importantly, I've learned to maintain self-respect and hold my head up during adversity. Chances are I will be judged more critically as a woman and sometimes misunderstood. I just have to work through it.

Regardless of the thought-provoking, seemingly surreal endeavor ahead of me, I have a lot of preparations to do before I leave the country for a year. Actually, I was preparing before I was even offered the job. I knew that once the interview process convened I'd only have a few weeks to get on a plane and go. I have a mortgage, a dog, a cat, a vehicle, paperwork, auto pay, prewritten permissions, notifications to insurance, credit cards, and banks. There are many responsibilities to consider.

I spoke with both chiefs six months ago and told them I would be applying for a fire job in Iraq, but I still have to request permission for a leave of absence. I only have a couple of weeks to put my whole life on hiatus mode until I return in one year.

I don't think I've ever been so organized in my life. My personal belongings are packed up in boxes and stored in the garage to make room for renters to move in. I notified all appropriate agencies and feel confident that all loose ends are tied up before my departure.

All right, I'm leaving the country and heading toward the unknown. I've been working on this for a while, but now more than ever, I realize that I need to get right with The Good Man Above.

I went to church when I was young, but I was uncomfortable when people spoke about the Lord outside church. I thought they were strange. It might have been my desire to fit in with the crowd at a vulnerable and impressionable age, or maybe it was just that I didn't know differently.

When I went to church as a young girl, I felt that God was calling me to utilize my love of singing to become part of the church choir. I constantly felt that calling, but I would've been way too embarrassed to actually do it. Those people up on stage were showing emotion and passion in a way that I was unfamiliar with. So I had this strange combination of a desire to do something and a simultaneous strong opposition.

I stopped going to church after a young age. It wasn't until recently I attended services again. With negativity swirling in the air, I needed to be surrounded by a positive environment. I made a dedication that I would attend church every Sunday, as long as I'm not on shift. I sat by myself in the pews, searching for strength and confidence to depend on no one else but God. I felt weird at first, just going alone.

I was new to this church and didn't know anyone, but I felt welcomed. Again, there was a pull on my heart to join the choir. I'm a strong woman; I know who I am now, and I don't need to impress everyone else. So if it's "uncool" to anyone, I've already dismissed their disapproval. I've been beaten down and gotten up enough times to realize that I only need to impress me. I followed my heart and took on the calling of joining the choir at the Mountain View Church.

I practice on Wednesday nights and sing on Sunday mornings. If my work shift falls on a Wednesday night, my captain lets me take the utility truck and a hand-held radio to church so I can practice with my group.

My fellowship with this group is invigorating. I'm loved and accepted without judgment. I've never been around a group of people so peaceful, loving, and kind. They model a character that I aspire to imitate—the epitome of God's light shining through human beings on earth.

When my choir group found out about my interest in traveling to Iraq to be a firefighter on a military base, they prayed over me that I would be guided for answers as to whether or not I should take the journey.

I pray daily for direction, and I find constant and unwavering affirmation, in the form of peace, that I am to follow through with this endeavor.

Chapter 5

Texas

In an unknown amount of days, I will be on a sixteen-hour flight to Dubai, then to Baghdad. Although I understand the general plans, there's no exact itinerary, and there're no airplane tickets except a one-way ticket from Portland, Oregon, to Houston, Texas. The mission is to work in Iraq as a firefighter for one year.

Over the last couple of years, I've been thinking about this adventure. I've prayed for guidance and my heart continually pulls me in the direction to go. I love my life at home—my own house, a dog, a cat, a big yard, great neighborhood, awesome friends, and an amazing job where I work twenty-four on/forty-eight off. My life is comfortable, and from a materialistic standpoint, life appears great. Regardless, I can't deny this longing to push myself out of my comfort zone, discover something new, and see the world. With significant convincing, I was approved for a one-year leave of absence from my job and should return to my normal life when I come home.

Although my family is afraid, they gave me well wishes and lots of hugs as I headed off to the airport on my big journey.

I just arrived in Houston, Texas, with my one-way ticket, so here I am. This scenario momentarily reminds me of an Internet scam where a woman flies solo to a different state and ends up in a dark alley. The fear of the unknown only briefly crosses my mind and then I'm back to my feelings of excitement and nervous anticipation.

It's the end of May and I went from the mild, Midwest, crispy, cool air to being struck in the face by humidity and ninety-degree heat. This weather causes me to sweat almost instantly when exiting the air-conditioned fuselage of the airplane. My jeans feel like they're stuck to me with perspiration, and I'm a little irritable until I remember that my destination will be far more uncomfortable than this. I mentally stop complaining about my current discomfort and accept the situation.

A hotel shuttle takes me to where I will meet the company of other travelers heading to Iraq as firefighters. I'm dropped off at a fancy hotel with a large foyer covered by marble flooring. There are gardens of green vegetation separating the mass of the large room and sporadically scattered nooks with seating, as if to invite for a long insightful conversation with a new companion.

The concierge directs me to a room at the end of the foyer. It appears dark and empty from the view of the bright, sunlit room that I'm currently in.

As I enter the dark room, I notice it's a billiard room. I'm acknowledged by approximately fifteen young men who sit around on chairs and pool tables with legs dangling off the sides. They are entrenched in conversation that leads me to realize that some of them have already been overseas and are acquainted with one another. They direct me to a pile of baggage where I drop off my suitcase and backpack.

I'm intimidated by the new crowd but reach a hand out with confidence and introduce myself to a few of the closest guys. "I'm Lizzy," I state while producing the appropriate-strength handshake to show self-assurance without trying to act overconfident or dominative. They reciprocate my handshake in the same fashion with a nod of the head and a quick introduction. I sit quietly, gauging my surroundings and taking in the various personalities and conversations of those around me. I hear several different accents among the group. There are Southern twangs, Midwest twists, and deep South drawls. It's apparent we're as mixed of an American variation as a hoarder's household collection. Of course, I feel as if I'm the only one without an accent.

One guy seems to be doing most of the talking. He jokes about a chief at one of the bases over in Iraq and everyone laughs. Only a couple of the guys know who he's talking about, but everyone laughs at his stories anyway, for camaraderie's sake. Even I laugh a little, not knowing to whom he's referring.

Gradually, we all join in conversations of inquiry as to where everyone is from. There are firefighters from Tennessee, Minnesota, North Carolina, New Jersey, Alabama, Mississippi, Missouri, Virginia, Pennsylvania, Iowa, Texas, and Washington—me. After a while, a man from Idaho joins us, so I'm no longer the only accent-less person from the western side.

Several of the guys are heading overseas for the first time, just like me, and some were there previously and able to give us insight on the project. We follow them around and listen to them with wide, inquisitive eyes, as if to sponge up as much information as possible. None of us "new guys" know what to expect with Iraq.

We still have a lot of time until our coordinator shows up, so the guys decide to get a drink at the bar on the other side of the hotel lobby. Some are already sharing a case of beer in the billiards room.

"We're not gonna get to drink for a year over there, so we might as well drink now!" exclaims one of the Southern boys.

I'm cautious as I follow them to the bar with a different perspective in mind. I'm not going to get obliterated prior to my departure, and I'm one woman among men. I need to maintain a level of self-control to solidify the intentions of my journey. I think one beer will be great, and I'll stop at that.

I sit on a bar stool next to "Bama," from Alabama, Rusty from Missouri, and a few others. These boys have the thickest accents I've ever heard, and their speech is starting to slur from beverage consumption.

I take the last drink of my Hefeweisen, foam and all. I set the bottle down on the cocktail napkin.

"You need another one. It's on me," Bama declares as he sets his own empty beer bottle down.

I smile politely and shake my head. "No thanks." I crinkle my nose and proceed to tell him, "That's all I'm gonna have."

Another guy at the bar lifts his beer up as a combination of a celebratory gesture and a way to indicate he has input to the conversation. "Aww, come on, Lizzy. You can handle one more."

I notice I'm being put on the spot in a similar fashion to one who's out for a night of drinking.

I sit up tall to show my confidence. "I know I can handle my alcohol, but I don't need to prove that to you."

"Ooh-hoo, she told you!" A deep voice rings in from the group.

Besides my intentions of focusing on my journey ahead, it's only been a month since my twenty-eighth birthday, where I can only assume I directly encountered GHB during a night out on the town. GHB is the fancy science term for Rohypnol, or roofies—aka the date-rape drug.

Since it was my birthday and I was meeting up with my girlfriends, I took extra time to look good. We were going to town for the evening and I wanted to feel confident and sassy. I wore a sexy, gray, pinstriped fedora, complete with the perfect makeup and curly, blonde pigtails. My friends and I occupied an ocean-view seat at a luxurious restaurant for dinner, followed by a drive downtown to see what other venues appeared inviting. Of all the places we could've chosen, we visited an old, hole-in-the-wall bar.

The bar was small but busy with a younger crowd. Music thumped through the old rattling walls and could be heard from the streets. Even though it smelled dingy, the inebriated crowd didn't seem to mind. Five other ladies and I took a seat at the tall, pub-style table in the corner and were instantly the center of attention. Men in their twenties' lingered over our table, hoping to start conversations. I don't mind conversation, but I think they had something else in mind from what I did. My girlfriends were soaking up the attention and laughing with all their new guy friends. The guys found out it was my birthday and started buying shots. I kept close tabs on my alcohol intake and discretely pushed full shots of Jager and other potent sugary concoctions to the side.

I drank a little bit to be social, but something wasn't right. I felt a dark tunnel closing in. I felt sick and was fading fast even though I only consumed a small amount of alcohol. I called up my buddy

Gabe—or Gabriel as I call him—and asked if I could stay at his place because it was closer than mine. I didn't want to catch a ride all the way to my house at the other end of the county.

I heard Gabe's voice on the other end of the line, always positive and happy to hear from me. "Of course, you can," he replied accommodatingly.

Everything went black in my memory. I have a slight recollection of my friends helping me to their car. I wouldn't have been able to walk on my own.

The next thing I knew, I was waking up at my buddy's house and the sun was up. A tall, trim, blond-haired Gabriel stood at the foot of the bed. He was dressed in his navy-blue fire department uniform, looking all official. He had to go to work early. "Are you going to be okay?" he asked.

I shook my head and looked down at my pants. I was wearing different clothing. "I don't remember anything."

Gabe shot me a sympathetic smile. "Well, give me a call later and let me know how you're feeling," he insisted.

I thanked him for taking me in to his home in such a condition. He allowed me to stay there as long as I needed.

It was a torturous day. I was in bed, in pain and unable to swallow the smallest drop of water without vomiting it out. As soon as I woke up and saw that my clothes were different and lost a chunk of my memory, I thought for sure I had been drugged.

When I gained enough strength, I called my doctor and scheduled an appointment to get my blood drawn.

I cringed as I sat up in bed and tried to listen to the woman on the phone. My head hurt too much to hear anyone speak. "Unfortunately, GHB doesn't remain in your blood for very long, so it might be undetectable at this point. We can get you an appointment and test your blood just in case. We can also look for any other possible substances."

"Okay," I replied. I scheduled the appointment for later in the day.

Around 4:00 p.m., I ate a couple of crackers without throwing up and was able to stand up for a few seconds at a time, which I couldn't do earlier. Gabe's roommate was home and drove me to get my Jeep so I could make it to my appointment.

When I called Gabe, he informed me that I was a rag doll that night when my friends dropped me off. I had no ability to take care of myself. There was vomit on my pants so he changed me out of my jeans into a pair of his sweatpants. He put a bucket next to the bed and was afraid to go to sleep because he didn't want me to aspirate on my own vomit. He didn't get much sleep that night while he watched over me.

I laughed a bit in embarrassment and confusion when he told me all of this. I had zero recollection of any of that and know that I didn't drink enough to get myself to that point. I'm so lucky to have him for a friend. It seems rare for a woman to feel trusting of a man in that circumstance, and I absolutely trust him with my life. I'm thankful for his friendship.

My blood tests showed up negative for GHB. The doctor tilted her head and raised her eyebrows at me. "It sounds possible that you consumed GHB, but it doesn't last in the blood stream long enough to test. You were lucky to be with trustworthy friends."

Back in Texas, our coordinator finally shows up with a van to shuttle us from Houston to College Station where we will be spending the week training for our Airport Rescue Firefighter (ARFF) certification.

We retrieve our bags from the billiards room and notice Bama is passed out on the floor.

"If they see him like this, he'll get sent home," one of the guys says. With a little coercion, a few people are able to get Bama up and pretending to be sober. We all hop in the van and head to our hotel in College Station.

Our five-day Airport Rescue Firefighter training is at the TEEX disaster training facility. Most of us will be stationed at fire departments near airfields in Iraq and we'll need to know how to respond to flight emergencies.

We start off with classroom lecture, and I feel thankful to be in an air-conditioned classroom, out of the Texas heat that I am so unaccustomed to. The heat, however, really is a good step toward acclimation of what is yet to come over in the Middle East.

We choose our seats in the classroom and anticipate the arrival of our instructors. In strut a few gentlemen. They are firefighters from the College Station Fire Department and the nearby airport fire station. The three instructors are physically all very different. One man is tall and slender. Another is a large, sturdy Italian man with a last name reminiscent of a popular Italian food. The third man is the most petite firefighter I've ever seen. Some of my traveling companions comment that he is "cute" when making reference to his size.

The three men are very good at what they do and size makes no difference in their abilities. They are knowledgeable and personable.

Throughout the classroom period, we obtain a plethora of information about airplanes, helicopters, airports, and runways. Airport firefighting is very different from structural firefighting in many ways and I didn't realize some of the details that needed to be taken into account. We learn about the colors, locations, and spacing of runway lights, the angle of approach to avoid inevitable flying parts, knowledge of the cockpit buttons that extinguish fires and shut down engines, and so much more. It's stimulating to learn new facts to add to my knowledge base.

The protective bunker gear utilized in aircraft firefighting is silver and is made to withstand the greater heat that is experienced in proximity to a large metal aircraft containing much fuel.

Besides the full-scale, metal airplane prop outside our classroom, there is a whole area with almost every training environment for any natural disaster one could think of. This is like a dream theme park for firefighters and other rescue personnel. Props are available for training in oil refinery fires, ship fires, building collapse, trench rescue, rope rescue, train wreck, and parking garage collapse. It's spectacular!

Along with a written final for our class, we're prepared for a whole day of live fire training on the airplane props. After a week of muggy, hot days, a storm rolls in. An ominous blur of haze washes in as the wind leads a downpour of rain. We are all dressed in our rental bunker gear and ready to fight some fire. Because the airplane prop is a large metal object, we're on the lookout for lightning, which will bring a swift end to our day of firefighting. We want to avoid electrocution, of course.

Surrounding the airplane is a lagoon of water about six inches deep. In order to approach the prop, we have to take a step down into the water and trudge forward with hose lines, a ladder, and any other equipment. We stand out in the monsoon as the E3 fuel is poured from the airplane's engines and lit with fire. We jump back, startled, as a fireball blasts out of the airplane engine. The explosion cascades out ten yards and whips up seven feet like an angry dragon tail. The radiant heat is intense even at a distance.

As the fire continues to rage, we are prompted to take our attack lines and proceed toward the inferno. We're partnered up two people per hose line. The hose pressure on our attack lines is intense so we bear down with a strong stance and tight grip while making purposeful movements inward. The large volume of water from our attack lines isn't defeating the fiery dragon. The flames spit out, pour down, and hover around the engine like a swarm of angry bees protecting their nest.

My partner and I ladder the airplane to make internal entrance as the other crew holds tight to their fire attack. Inside the structure, there are seats in rows just as you would see in any airplane, but these are metal. Bales of scattered hay are lit on fire, creating a very real environment of heat and smoke. Our mission is search and rescue. We find the victims (which are dummies) and begin extrication while utilizing the light from the fire, then we extinguish the fire. This method is all backward to us as structural firefighters. Typically, we attempt to extinguish the flames at first sight to control the primary threat. In this case, extinguishing the flames first causes a hot metal tunnel of burning steam and total darkness.

The entire class gets an opportunity to rotate through the scenarios multiple times and the fire burns almost continuously from the engines throughout the day, giving us a great show and some heat to help us stay warm. With the deep water under our boots and rain from above, our bunker gear and underlying clothing are saturated. I feel like I've been playing in a water park all day while wearing my fire gear.

Celebration time! The finale of our ARFF class comes with a night out on the town in College Station. We lounge at a rooftop bar and sip on beer while the sun goes down over Texas. The evening is mellow as we sit on outdoor furniture and prop up our feet on the metal table supports.

As the sun sets over yonder and the beer starts settling, we begin to notice the absence of our travel companion.

"Where's Bama?" someone asks.

We scurry to the edge of the rooftop and glance over the side. No Bama in sight. We decide it's time to locate our dear friend whom we've grown close to over this crazy week. I have a nagging worry that he's passed out alone somewhere.

Red and blue lights flash off the cement walls and illuminate a darkened alley. We round the corner and spot a policewoman standing over Bama. She peers down at him while he sits propped against the building. He has a goofy, inebriated grin on his face, legs straight out in front, and limp upper body.

The ambulance has arrived. A white and blue fire engine cruises by to glance at the scene. If Bama was unconscious, they would need the engine crew to help revive him. This isn't the circumstance at all; he's simply waking up from a drunken slumber.

The officer plans to haul Bama off to the big house for the night.

We plead with the officer on his behalf. "Ma'am, please. We're leaving to Iraq in a couple of days and we're catching a van back to the hotel right now. Let us just take him."

The officer stares at us with a stoic expression. She's unimpressed and has probably heard every excuse in the book. She then bites her lip and contemplates the situation. "Okay, you guys need to leave now though, before I change my mind."

Our van pulls up just a short time after. On the ride back to the hotel, we joke with Bama about his encounter with the law and how he almost spent the evening in a cement bedroom. He thanks us for "having his back," and we're pretty proud of ourselves for mitigating the situation as well.

We return to Houston after our week of certification in College Station. Upon arrival, we discover that there are about twenty more firefighters joining our group. Most of these guys are returners and already have their certifications for airport firefighting. I'm surprised to learn that many of them are prior military and were firefighters in the air force, army, and marines.

While in Houston, we spend another whole week in classroom training to prepare for entrance into Iraq, which is now termed a "hostile environment." They don't like to say it's a "war zone." It's all about using the appropriate verbiage to create a particular illusion to people on the outside.

The training consists of a lengthy section on "what to do if you become a prisoner of war." Being that we will not be leaving our base unless we're headed to Baghdad, or leaving the airport, I don't find myself too concerned about being in this predicament. There are contractors in the session that will be driving trucks in convoys across the country. This session seems quite a bit more applicable to them, but still very interesting to me.

We learn how to use tap code, which is similar to Morse code, but easier. If we were imprisoned and needed to carry conversations with another prisoner, we could tap out words without being understood by the enemies.

Our group leader tells us that three contract firefighters have died in Iraq. One death was a heart attack, which is the number one cause of firefighter deaths in America; another death was when a firefighter was being transported to his base in a convoy that struck an IED (improvised explosive device); the third death occurred when a hollowed-out rocket was used as a cigarette-butt disposer. It's common for members of the military to use previously detonated mortars as such a disposal device, but they are deep cleaned and all explosive residue is removed. In this case, the young man did not have a cleaned-out rocket shell; the blasting cap was still present. The lit cigarette butt was tossed into the rocket shell, which made contact with the blasting cap and created a reaction. He had enough time to realize something wasn't right so he grabbed the volatile shell and tried to run away from the firehouse to save the rest of the firefighters. The rocket exploded in his hands and he was killed instantly. Although he did not make it, his quick reaction saved the lives of those who were around him.

After our long days of training for entrance into Iraq, we find entertainment in catching a Houston Astros baseball game, eating fried pickles and drinking beer at the Laundromat, and roaming around Wal-Mart. Now it's in the plans to hit up a country-western bar.

We have the hotel concierge call a taxi to pick us up and take us to the bar for the evening. Our IDs are checked, and we pass through the doors to enter a darkened room, lit only by fluorescent beverage propaganda.

Clothing attire is diverse with a large representation of folks wearing cowboy hats and boots with Wranglers. Our crew is fairly casual with jeans and T-shirts. I'm sticking to my casual look with a pair of jeans, a purple top, and a pair of Romeos, which are essentially leather slip-on shoes that look like boots. I omitted the application of makeup for tonight, as I have for my whole time in Texas so far. I don't desire to attract any attention from my male counterparts on this adventure.

We hang around as a group for a while, shouting condensed versions of conversations over the loud music. Eventually, we catch on to the dance mode and a few of the guys take me out on the floor and insist I learn how to two-step.

Around and around on the dance floor we go, in sync with the crowd of couples also putting forth their best feet. All are on beat with the music, and every once in a while, an experienced dance couple floats on by, adding extra twirls to augment the same old moves that we are executing. I have never been taken out dancing like this before. I love the country music in the background while being treated like a lady out on the dance floor.

I have only lightly acquainted with the new group of firefighters that arrived in Houston after us. Although we have all barely met, we get along as if we're long-time friends. We corral in the upstairs foyer between our rooms to talk about the upcoming travel to Dubai, and curiosity piques in regards to which base we will be individually stationed at.

While leaning up against the window ledge, I engage in a casual conversation with Alex. He previously served in Iraq while in the air force. He's now returning as a contracted lieutenant firefighter. Alex is Hispanic, with beautiful, dark-brown skin and amazing dark eyes. He was born and raised in Texas, but both of his parents were from Mexico, so he speaks fluent Spanish and English. Something about his look was intimidating to me when I first saw him, but as soon as he cracked a smile, he seemed very sweet. This is the first conversation I've had with him since his group arrived this week.

I find myself impressed with him. Not only is he intelligent and articulate, but I can sense that he's a strong leader. I'm hopeful to be at the same base as him because he would be a good mentor and challenge me to become a better firefighter. Although he has me intrigued, our conversation is strictly business. I'm not interested in starting any type of relationship at this time.

I know that I may never see Alex again because he already has all the paperwork to return to Iraq quickly. The rest of us have waiting periods for our entrance visas, and additional training in Baghdad.

Chapter 6

Dubai

OUR NEWLY CLOSE-KNIT GROUP HAS been disbanded and disbursed onto different airlines, at different times, and on different days. There are five other people on my flight from the group. We flew from Houston to Atlanta and next will fly to Dubai.

Boarding the Delta flight from Atlanta to Dubai, I'm not expecting comfort. I suspected I would be seated coach in a narrow, middle seat. I was correct. Squeezing through the aisle, I reach my assigned middle seat and settle in to make the best of the sixteen-hour flight. I pull out the Sky Mall catalog and start browsing through pages. I'm always entertained with the unique gift ideas in this catalog. It's filled with "Why didn't I think of that?" inventions.

A woman startles me with her sudden appearance as she leans over to talk to me. The woman approaches me with an aggressive demeanor, but I don't think she's being rude; she just seems to have a strong presence. She asks me—actually, she demands—I trade seats with her son. She wants him to sit next to her. Well, no seat can be worse than a middle seat in coach so I'm not particularly attached to my own. I'm happy to oblige.

The woman directs me where to go and as I walk up the aisle, I see that the seat is an exit row, aisle seat. Wow! What luck!

The long flight passes by fairly quickly. Dare I say to my fellow travelers that this actually isn't that bad? I have all the legroom I can possibly handle, the people next to me are friendly, and each seat has its own personal TV with movies and shows to choose from. I spend two of the sixteen hours watching *"The Blind Side"* with Sandra Bullock—such a good movie.

I realize now that we weren't told how long we will be in Dubai. Will we be there for a few hours or a couple of days? I also remember back to all the training we received this week about "incoming," terrorism, human trafficking, IEDs, and what to do, in detail, on a day-to-day basis to keep mentally healthy if you find yourself captured by terrorists.

I drift asleep and have a dream that we're in Baghdad for our one-week processing and we experience several indirect fires (IDF) from outside the base. I try to dodge the incoming explosive devices but I keep getting hit. The bombs are hitting me no matter where I run, but they're not exploding, just clinging to me. I'm awoken suddenly by turbulence while vivid images from my dream still linger. I've had very little apprehension about this journey, but the turbulence wakes me in fear.

Dubai is a large and wealthy city in the United Arab Emirates (UAE), located southeast of Saudi Arabia by the Persian Gulf. It's known for its unique architecture, palm tree-shaped island, the tallest building in the world, great international shopping, camels, the sport of falconry, desert sand floating in the Arabian sky, and other mysterious and sacred cultural arts.

Because this is a Muslim nation, the "call to prayer" echoes over the city from the loud speakers of mosques five times a day. It's an a cappella voice singing in Arabic with a smooth, calm tone and strong vibrato. At specific times during the day, the religious tune is sung over the speakers at the mall, the airport, and any other large area where people congregate. There are prayer rooms accessible in many areas for the Muslims who follow this strict ritual. People drop whatever they're doing and join the prayer.

The local nationals are easy to decipher from the rest of the population in the UAE. The men wear white robes called *kanduras*, and they're always pristine and wrinkle free. Their headscarf is typically red and white checkered pattern. The women wear long, black robes called abayas and headscarves to cover their hair and sometimes burqas to cover their faces. Many times the women will only show their eyes and hands while everything else is completely hidden in black material. Sometimes, the black robes and scarves are covered in jewels.

Modesty is held in high regards for this culture. In fact, the laws here are so strict that you could be put in jail if caught kissing your own spouse in public.

While en route to our hotel from the airport, we're briefed of an 11:00 p.m. to 7:00 a.m. curfew in Dubai but told that it isn't really upheld anymore. We're also briefed on several other very strict laws that are enforced in this country.

Once we enter the lobby, we glimpse a few familiar faces. Big smiles are exchanged as we acknowledge the other group who has arrived just prior to us. We act as if we haven't seen them in forever and that it's such a coincidence to meet up with them randomly on this side of the world, in this exact hotel. But really, we're all going to end up in this same hotel so it's not so dramatic.

Our two groups combine and set out to view the evening streets of Dubai. The time zone is completely opposite here. We decide on Burger King for dinner even though I just woke up and recently consumed my morning coffee at the end of the flight. I order a chicken sandwich and give the woman twenty US dollars. In return, she gives me fifty dirham and a coin. The exchange rate is approximately 3.5 dirhams per dollar.

We sit down to eat and observe the pedestrians strolling outside. Many wear long white robes and head pieces. The cultural diversity here is a site. Bollywood music videos blare from a nearby television along with American songs from Usher and Rihanna.

We consume our meals under the humming, fluorescent lights of the fast-food venue. Next, we will attend a nightclub, knowing that this could be risky. If Americans are seen drunk in public, under

Islamic law, we can be arrested immediately. The United States has a separation of church and state, but here if you offend their religious beliefs you break their law.

The sound of a booming band greets us as we enter the little nightclub. The room is almost too dark to even see while walking over to sit at the table. I decide not to drink while a few others order only a beer. We're all a little bit paranoid to drink, so even the guys that order a beer are trying to share theirs with those of us who didn't order anything.

I just can't stop staring at the girls on stage with this band. These two girls are probably in their early twenties' and I imagine they're from the Philippines. They appear to be drugged out of their minds. They're wearing skimpy, bright-colored outfits that barely cover their thin little thighs. Some moments, they're jumping around and dancing to the music, and next, they're standing motionless as if they have no clue where they are. I feel saddened for these young women. What's their story? Why are they here?

Human trafficking and prostitution are prevalent in Dubai. When Americans go out of their hotels, they are often swarmed by prostitutes offering up their services. These prostitutes are not necessarily offering themselves because it's their desire to do so. For many, it's because their life depends upon it. People who purchase these services only further the succession of the human trade and the detriment it creates to human life.

During our many training sessions for traveling abroad, there was an issue that was highlighted over and over again; this was the concern for human trafficking. Human trafficking is a greater issue than many have yet to grasp. It's now being highlighted in the news more and more, but it's prevalent in every country, including the United States.

Human trafficking is the buying and selling of humans for cheap labor and/or sex. There's no discrimination among race, age, and gender. Victims are usually tricked and lured into these situations by promises of good-paying jobs or other great opportunities. They're then kidnapped and sold, sometimes very cheaply. Victims can be moved around so much that it's often untraceable to find them and their families may never see them again. They're typically forced to live in inhumane environments. Many are beaten and threatened harm to their families if they don't do as told.

I was told a story from a family of missionaries working in Thailand at an orphanage. They shared an experience about a thirteen-year-old girl who was very bright and happy. She had a strong love for God in her heart as well as great ambitions for her future. One day her biological mother came to the orphanage with a van full of armed men and abducted her by gunpoint. This bright young girl was sold for under a thousand dollars to a brothel in Bangkok. She was then shipped around from place to place for prostitution and was untraceable to save.

My eyes have been opened to the issue and I fear traveling alone in a place where I may stand out as a cultural or racial minority. I know there are locations I may also be a target for danger because I am an American.

I estimate it's about three in the afternoon at home, in Washington. I think it's about two or three in the morning here in Dubai and I'm wide-awake. The time change is messing with me. We left Houston, Texas, yesterday and flew for about sixteen hours—a little over 8,000 miles. I'm not even certain what day of the week it is right now. I'm in my hotel room watching Arabic music videos because there's nothing else to do. I wonder how everyone else is sleeping in their own rooms.

After a couple of hours, I manage to fall asleep and get a little bit of rest. I need energy so I can go out and discover more of the city. I'm excited to be in a foreign country, unique and different from anywhere I've ever been.

Today we're going to the Emirates Mall to go shopping. I'm tired of the boring clothes I packed, but there's really no point in buying anything cute. I probably won't need many clothes anyway because we'll wear a uniform every day in Iraq.

I don't have many clothing options with me, and it's so hot here. Because of the Middle Eastern heat, buildings are not filled with the heavy carpeting or tapestries but with marble flooring, light drapery, and other heat-reducing interior designs.

I'm getting ready for my day by organizing my personal belongings in the room and patting around bare foot to admire the smooth, cold marble under my feet. Obtaining the full experience of alternate architecture is romantic to me. Different textures, colors, and ambiances bring forth an exceptionally beautiful experience to the environment. There's no hurry to be anywhere except for breakfast down in the lobby, so I enjoy taking my time.

In the lobby, we congregate over a complimentary continental breakfast. Laughter surrounds the table when we discover that most of us were wide-awake and bored at 3:00 a.m., watching Arabic music videos. We could've gotten together and hung out if we knew that we were all awake.

Our breakfast is standard with a buffet of eggs, breads, waffles, and other foods. The only thing nontraditional to us is the coffee creamer. Instead of our typical cow's cream, the coffee is served with camel's milk. I love my morning coffee and I don't think there's any better way to start off the day. Coffee and camel's cream tastes exotic, yet customary. It takes my everyday habit to a unique level of pleasure.

After breakfast, we take a cab to the Emirates Mall. The mall is the best place to go for "people watching." We're so entrenched in Western culture that it's amusing to view a culture of people who are so modest and dress in relation to their religion. Why do we have the desire to stare at people who are different from us? It's as if subconsciously we think we can discover the mysteries of our differences, if we could only just look long enough. This area is multicultural and there are people from other areas of the Middle East and Asia and from all over the world.

The mall has a large indoor skiing arena with ski lifts and full snow gear rentals. We're all afraid to go skiing or snowboarding because we don't want to break a leg or arm right before starting a new fire job in Iraq. We peer through the large, glass windows and admire the man-made winter wonderland while forgetting it's over a hundred degrees outside.

Our day at the mall consists of clothing shopping, eating hummus at the food court, and scrounging through gift stores. I made a friend on this trip who isn't a firefighter; she's going to work at headquarters in Baghdad. Her name is Nim. Nim and I navigate through each layer of the mall together, checking out all the expensive purses and clothing. We spot a life-size bronze camel and stop to take Kodak moments of one another. In this testosterone-filled environment that I've been subjected to, it's nice to have another woman to chat with and take a break from the guys.

It seems as if the day passes quickly and we head back to our individual hotel rooms for a nap. Our bodies are so messed up from the time-zone flip. Daytime here is nighttime at home. All I want to do is sleep just a little more. Everyone likes the idea of getting some rest before dinner.

This evening I'm spending some time alone to reflect on recent excitement and ponder what the future has in store for me. I want to check out the view from the top of the building.

The air is heavy and warm as I step outside on the top deck of the hotel. The swimming pool flickers a golden reflection as if to beckon me in for a dip. *"Maybe later,"* I think as I acknowledge the cool temptation. It's peaceful up here and the sun is setting over the desert. I can see beyond the city boundaries where the vast, barren desert begins. The dust has rolled in across the city, lingering in a haze over skyscrapers. A light breeze pushes its way through the warmth and wisps through my hair as I watch a group of pigeons flit off the ledge into the orange sky. I'm unaccompanied on the balcony and it's quiet above the city streets, except for the "call to prayer" echoing calmly from a nearby mosque.

We still don't know how long we'll be staying in Dubai. We're waiting on approval from the government of Iraq with our entrance visas. A couple of people from our group were approved sooner than the rest and they were able to leave to Baghdad today. It looks like we have another day and night at the very least.

We hire a tour guide to check out the city and he drives us all around Dubai in a taxicab. We stop at several different spots including art museums, flea markets, the world's tallest building, Atlantis, and the beach by the Persian Gulf. At the markets, they sell spices, sugared dates, and Persian tapestries.

During the drive, our guide talks about the nearby mosques and points out the homes that belong to the families of the wealthy rulers. We see the palm tree-shaped island that was built on top of the water. It's an amazing spectacle. The trunk of the palm tree and all the palm fronds extend off land into the sparkling waters of the Persian Gulf.

Midway through our half-day tour, the drowsiness of jetlag hits me hard and I struggle to stay conscious. I try everything I can to overcome the jetlag but again I was up at 3:00 a.m. watching Arabic music videos last night. My eyelids are like heavy anvils pulling downward from gravity. I don't want to be rude to our tour guide but the situation is out of my control. I'm tired! Drowsiness is frustrating when you want to enjoy your surroundings.

Back at the hotel, I enjoy a dip in the pool and I'm joined by some of the other firefighters. We find out that we'll be flying out early the next morning, and we're anxious to get going. The experienced travelers give us the rundown on what to expect at Baghdad International Airport. Things have changed a lot over the last few years, and the Iraqi's are back in complete control of their airport. We have to abide by their rules.

Chapter 7

Arriving in Baghdad

Baghdad International Airport (BIAP)—we're finally in Iraq. Our large group of American contractors is herded off the tarmac and placed in lines in the back entrance of the airport. The Iraqi men working at BIAP are dressed in pressed, white, button-up shirts and black slacks. Some of the men stand casually behind the ticket counter in a swirl of white cigarette smoke as they stare out at us with one eye while taking a long drag on the white stick. It reminds me of something from a 1980's movie, being that I haven't seen people smoke indoors since that era. In Washington, where I'm from, it's illegal to smoke inside businesses.

They call us forward one line at a time and we cooperate with every request. Our passports are handed over to the Iraqi man with hazel eyes, who methodically stacks our personal documents on top of each other. We wait for several minutes as they take our stacked passports and paperwork into a different room. After a while, the man returns and calls out our names to hand us our passports. I take my passport from the man and flip open the pages to peer at my first visa. It's a big sticker that takes up the whole page and has a falcon and Arabic writing. I find myself pleased with my new travel souvenir.

We caravan away from BIAP in large buses with curtains over the windows. I feel intimidated in my new surroundings and unsure of the level of safety at hand. Without speaking to my first-timer friends, I can almost palpate the shared uncertainty and apprehension.

I had no idea what Iraq was going to look like, even though I've seen movies. I didn't picture it to have much vegetation. I'm surprised that there are palm trees everywhere, with areas of green vegetation in sparse patches across the clay-colored desert sand. The sky is cloudless and blue with a temperature of 127 degrees Fahrenheit. The radiating, dry heat is comparable to a convection oven or a large hair dryer when accompanied with a steady wind gust. Military Black Hawks fly overhead in pairs, propellers beating at the wind with each revolution. I've arrived to the desert and I can hardly believe I'm actually, really here in Baghdad, Iraq.

My mood at this point is an obnoxious concoction of nervous energy, anticipation, excitement, and lethargy from leaving my comfortable hotel room in Dubai at 0100 (1:00 a.m.). Maybe they'll let us take a nap since we're all jetlagged and desperately overcome with exhaustion.

The bus drops us off and we're told to check in to our living quarters where we'll stay for the week and finish up our entrance training.

My room is in a little white trailer packed with three bunk beds to house six women at a time. The guys are staying in large military tents with sleeping bags on top of twin-size beds.

"Is it nap time yet?" we all question.

We meet the lieutenant who is in charge of our training for the week, and he tells us that we need to meet in the training tent after we check in to our housing. We had two busy weeks in Texas for ARFF training, "Iraqi war zone" preparations, and partying, followed by three days of drowsiness in Dubai, and a 0100 (1:00 a.m.) wake time for our flight to Baghdad. Now we're going straight to classroom training?

It's our first day in Baghdad and we're immediately scheduled on a full day of classroom training: "death by PowerPoint." We sit on wooden picnic-style benches in a tent and this person at the front of the room is just talking and talking. I look around the tented room through droopy, half-open eyes to see if anyone else is struggling to stay awake as much as I am. *"Please don't let me be the only one,"* I think. Half the class is asleep on the table, and the other half is nodding off while concentrating on holding heavy eyelids open.

I drift asleep and my body falls backward. I wake up startled and catch my torso mid fall, just before hitting my head on the wooden table behind me. *"Concentrate, Lizzy. 'Don't be rude to the presenter,"* I self-encourage. I'm in need of a little self-pep talk now.

I wake up and lift my heavy head from off my folded hands. I don't even remember falling asleep! The instructor just keeps on talking. He doesn't quit speaking or change his pace or his tone. The topics were about safety and ... I can't even recall what else because I was sleeping.

After the torturous classroom experience, we are set free for dinner. In parting words from our instructor, our exhaustion is acknowledged as he states that the plan all along was to purposely keep us up in this torturous fashion in order to combat jetlag. Now I don't feel so bad for being a poor student today.

As we tread off to the dining facility (DFAC) for our meal, we meander between tall maze-like cement barriers and trudge through ankle-twisting gravel that crunches under our boots. There are numerous tunnels made of cement and sandbags. If a mortar is shot onto base, we can hide there for protection. Large pallets with hundreds of unlabeled twenty-ounce water bottles sit almost every one hundred yards and are covered in the fine powdery dirt from the ground.

The T-wall cement barriers are everywhere on base, protecting living quarters and anywhere that people will congregate. The thickly layered gravel is awkward for a path covering, but a purposeful feature. Since the desert sand is a fine dirt-like powder that turns into a sticky mud in the rainy winter months, the large amounts of gravel are necessary to keep the mud from caking up on our boots like peanut butter. We're told the sticky mud is difficult to remove, even with copious amounts of pressurized water.

We arrive to the DFAC and stand in the sweltering sun along with all the military personnel, contractors, and third-country nationals (TCN). Our ID badges are checked closely by the Ugandan guards who are dressed from head to toe in desert-tan combat-style uniform. They stand at the entrances with their AK-47s on shoulder and look carefully at the photo on each badge while comparing to our faces. If we wear sunglasses, they make us remove them so they can get a really good look at our face. This will be the routine every single day, for every single meal.

One of the veteran firefighters from our group tells us a story about the Ugandan guards actually popping off a shot into the rear of a marine as he entered the DFAC because he wouldn't cooperate with their security procedures. I'm intimidated by the thought.

Everyone corrals into a little room filled with sinks. Thorough hand washing is expected before entering the DFAC. Next, we retrieve a cafeteria tray and plastic silverware. There are a few different food options and enough calories to keep anyone from starving. All the while, we're still receiving points of wisdom from our companions who have more experience.

"Only eat dessert on Sundays," one of the guys says. "You'll gain weight if you're not careful."

All the men and women in the military are required to keep their weapons with them at all times, even when sitting down to eat. An arsenal of M16 and M4 rifles blanket the tiled floor, under the long dining tables, while the service members take a break from their diligent duties. Some wear army or air force combat uniform with camouflage jacket and pants, while some wear physical training uniform with shorts and a T-shirt. The military presence is comprised mostly of army and air force personnel, and occasionally a marine presence. The marine presence was a lot greater during the earlier years of the war in Iraq when there were more combat missions.

As the sun is setting, we take our full bellies away from the DFAC and head to the PX (military grocery store) to buy some hygienic necessities. I purchase what I need and begin to head back to my sleeping quarters.

It's my first night on base and I find myself alone after sunset and starting to get lost in the cement jungle of T-wall mazes. I begin to panic as I recall my chronic inability to maintain a sense of good direction. There are very few landmarks in the maze, and only a few makeshift light poles to assist me. Everything looks the same, and it's dark out here! Mosquitoes are swarming and a few bats flap about searching for their dinner. *"I can't get lost,"* I think. *"I don't wanna run into a bad guy, and I also don't wanna be embarrassed for getting lost."*

No one is around and it would be a quiet evening in the desert, if it weren't for the loud rocks crushing to the tempo of my every panicked footstep. I crunch around in my heavy boots and proceed around a dark corner. A tall figure appears and I jump back startled. My sudden fear turns into comfort as I realize it's just one of the guys from my group. He's been to Baghdad many times and knows his way around. I confess that I'm lost and need a little help finding my way back. He walks with me and then points out the simple directions for my safe return to the women's housing unit. Although I'm embarrassed, he gives me no flack, just the help I need to find my way.

During our week in Baghdad, we spent many hours in training and acclimation. We spent several hours under the sweltering sun while taking turns with the driving course, and had a three-day certification course in telecommunications. The telecommunication course is required so that we can rotate through dispatch positions at our own bases where we will receive emergency calls and dispatch the appropriate fire and EMS response.

Everywhere we went, we were walking outside in the heat of the day. By the end of the week, while sitting in the back of our tent classroom, I saw the beautifully browned necks of my cohorts from having spent many hours in the desert sun.

In my little white trailer, I had seven different roommates that came and went throughout the week. Most of the women just stayed there for one night, sometimes two or three. They were passing through Baghdad either to their base or back to Dubai. Half the people staying there have jetlag because they're returning from the United States, so sleep was difficult for all.

I'm still waking up in the middle of the night and have yet to get a full night's sleep. I then have to walk about one hundred yards outside to get to the women's latrine.

The bathrooms are referred to as latrines on base, even though I'm sure 99 percent of the people here would normally call it a bathroom at home. Other than latrines, there are plenty of "Port-a-Johns" to accommodate any sudden circumstance along the walking routes. With all the water we've been guzzling, I frequent the latrines as often as possible so I don't have to use one of those blue, plastic "Port-a-John" cubicles. At 127 degrees Fahrenheit, it's miserable to sit inside, on a portable toilet seat where the temperature is probably twenty degrees higher. I'm already trying to grow accustomed to the constant inhabitants of sweat in every curvature and crevice of my body, so the idea of enclosing myself into a cubicle-like Petri dish of happy flourishing microorganisms is rather unpleasant.

The women's latrine nearest my CHU is also a white singlewide trailer. It has about six toilets, six shower stalls, and four sinks with mirrors. There were a few times when I was taking a shower and the power would shut down, leaving me in pitch darkness while the water would continue its typical fluctuation between scorching hot and breathtaking cold.

I've kind of enjoyed staying here because it reminds me of camping. Everyone that goes into the bathroom to brush their teeth in the morning has bags under their eyes and sports the "I've been camping out" look.

The latrine trailer is a busy little place and is up kept by a couple of nice Filipina women. There is one woman named Amy who is always working in the latrine area, cleaning the toilets and mopping the tiny floor. Amy has worked in Baghdad for about six years. Every time I see her, she has a huge smile on her face. It makes her day when people acknowledge her and treat her as if she's a long-time friend. She knows how to speak some English and does her best to converse with everyone.

"You are so beautiful," she would tell me every day when I smiled at her.

"No, *you* are beautiful!" I would reply.

She made me feel special with her kindness, and I hoped to return the favor.

When you work in Iraq, you don't usually get a day off. There's nothing to do if you have the day off, and the things that need to be done are done daily. I imagine that Amy has been working most days of the past six years doing the same thing, day in, day out. They don't call it Groundhog Day around here for nothing.

Our week in Baghdad is now coming to a finale and we are finally told which bases we will be individually assigned to. I find out that I'm assigned to Forward Operating Base Taji, which is just north of Baghdad and west of the Tigris River. I will have to fly by helicopter to get there. Many of the guys are stationed here on this base in Baghdad and will not need additional transportation, while some will have to fly by airplane to get to more distant locations.

The other day I met a firefighter named Lopez, who is stationed at Taji. He had to fly to Baghdad for a test that we do every year. I tried to introduce myself to him, since we will be living on the same base. He came across unfriendly and too good for my presence. I just found out we're scheduled to travel together to Taji, and I'm not really looking forward to it.

As we part ways from Baghdad and disperse to our individual bases around Iraq, my buddies T-Savage and Adam meet me near the transportation location to see me off. I'm already missing my new friends and wish I could take them with me, but I'm pleased with the respect they're showing me as we part ways. It seems like a transfer of respect is occurring because it shows this other guy, whom I just met, that I'm respected by those who I have spent time with during our training experience. After my friends say good-bye, I notice a slight change in Lopez's attitude toward me, which is good because we have a lot of waiting around this evening as we prepare to take our mil-air flight to Taji.

Daytime quickly turns to nighttime and all is silent as we wait patiently for the helos to arrive and take us to our destination. It's dark and warm outside and the bats are busy flapping around to eat up the obnoxious mosquitoes. The quiet stillness of the dark evening is suddenly penetrated by a faint sound of propellers in the distance. All pedestrians stand and pick up baggage in anticipation of the arrival.

To fly mil-air, we are required to wear bulletproof vests, Kevlar helmets, eye protection, and earplugs. Most people use their sunglasses as their required eye protection, which is a bad idea because it causes them to be visually impaired in the dark. We stand in a line like a herd of cattle when two huge Chinook choppers glide down onto the tarmac. The long body of the aircraft has two large propellers, one at each end. The first part of the group is hustled over to the first Chinook, and then I'm guided to proceed to the second. I step carefully, as I too am wearing my sunglasses in the dark. That was a bad idea.

With my earplugs in, I can still hear the loud beating of all four propellers hitting the wind, but not the man trying to give us verbal directions.

As we proceed closer to the Chinook, the wind force and heat from the jets becomes greater. By the time we reach the ramp to make entry, the powerful jets show their formidable strength as they blow a strong and steady heat blast through our hair and clothing. We hold on tightly to our baggage and move purposefully as to keep from staggering our gait against the force. The grandeur of the engine leaves me with a feeling of awe and excitement. I'm proud to have the opportunity to fly with the military in this magnificent apparatus.

This isn't a leisurely flight from Baghdad to Taji; this is the military doing us a favor and allowing us to come aboard with their cargo while they make pickups and deliveries to the other bases. They're courteous to us as they help load baggage and direct us to seats with our backs against the fuselage. Just as quickly as we are loaded, the Chinook elevates high above the tarmac and hovers in place. With a quick tilt laterally, the Chinook speeds forward into the dark.

I'm seated close to one of the circular windows and can view all the lights of Baghdad. The army crew has night-vision goggles secured to their faces. There's someone poised on lookout at every side. They're focused as they continuously scan the terrain below while positioned behind M16 rifles. The back ramp of the Chinook is wide open, creating a platform with an open view of the sky. The man in position toward the back straps on a harness to his belt and sits down on the open ramp to dangle his legs off the edge while peering down into the dark desert. *I would love to have that job,* I think.

After a few stops at other locations, we land in Taji, Iraq.

Chapter 8

Taji, Iraq

WE ARRIVE AT TAJI AIR Base in the evening and are picked up by my new chief.

"Hi, Lizzy," he says as we get in the battalion rig.

"Hi, Chief," I reply. There's no need for introductions; I'm the only female firefighter on this base for now.

"Yeah, we checked your Facebook page when we heard you were coming," Lopez comments.

Chief and Lopez describe the two fire stations on base and the differences between them. Station 2 is comprised of containerized housing units (CHU). There are usually two living areas connected to a bathroom, which is called a wet CHU. A dry CHU is a trailer without a bathroom attached. There's enough room for about eight people at station 2 and there's a fire engine and a water tanker that respond from there.

Station 1 is a hard-structure building next to the airfield with an apparatus bay attached. It has two long hallways for living quarters, with a small kitchen, living room, training room, a few offices, and a few bathrooms. This station can accommodate around twenty people under one roof, although I've heard that at random times they've been overstaffed and had to create modified sleeping arrangements.

Chief informs me that I will be at station 1, located on the south end of the base. I wanna see what this place looks like, but it's dark and I can only view what's in the headlights, the paved road in front of us, and the sandy dirt bordering the cement as we drive. This base seems so much different from Baghdad. It's more rural, dark, and desolate.

The apparatus bay at station 1 is lit up as we arrive. The structure is completely surrounded by T-walls, bunkers with sandbags, and Connex boxes.

We're quiet as we enter the station, trying not to wake anyone. The fluorescent lighting in the hallway hits my eyes, so I squint and turn away.

"Your room will be just down the hall here," Chief says in a quiet voice. "We should have it set up for the most part, but we'll need to find you a night stand tomorrow. Hope your mattress isn't too uncomfortable."

I enter my little nine-foot by nine-foot bedroom and only briefly acknowledge my surroundings. Feeling exhausted, I almost don't think my brain can handle any new information or stimulus at this point. I just need to rest and I'll adapt to any mattress. I'm thankful that such accommodations even exist. I had anticipated and prepared for the possibility of far less.

The springs on my single bed squeak as I climb on top of the old mattress and pull the sheets over my head. Regardless of the loud chirping cricket in my floor tile, I pass out quickly and sleep through the night.

Morning arrives and I hear the sounds of the other firefighters waking up, taking showers, and pumping up the music to get energized for the day. It feels as if I'm on a heavy dose of Dramamine. Tired and confused, I realize I need to get up to use the latrine.

In order to get to the female latrine, I walk down one hallway, turn the corner to another short hallway, and then walk past the day room. It's not a long trek, but the building is compact and I have to pass seven other bedrooms along the way. We're living in close quarters to accommodate everyone.

A couple of people stand around in the day room, drinking their morning coffee as I pass by. It's strange being the "new guy" in a place in which you will reside with others. Who introduces whom? Should I expect them to be the first to reach out a hand and welcome me into their home, or do I reach out and introduce myself out of respect for entering their home? I think either one works. It just becomes awkward when neither side facilitates that introduction, so I quickly decide that it's my job to step up to introductions. First impressions immediately come into play. The majority of the guys seem easygoing and welcoming while a couple of others give the impression that they need time to warm up to me. Their difference in personality doesn't matter much to me; either they will end up liking me or they won't.

In the firehouse, we're sometimes forced to spend time with people that we wouldn't normally associate with, let alone learn their name. You also get to know everybody's quirks, like it or not. Typically, you'll find multiple individuals who are of the type-A personality in this occupation—competitive and aggressive—but all types of personalities find their way into the firehouse. I've spent a lot of time around people who may be described as prickly or abrasive. When forced to be around someone like such, I enjoy discovering their weakness or soft side. Some of them secretly have some sort of passion for life and I find it endearing to witness the small moments that show their heart and makes their eyes sparkle.

I thought that my sleep deprivation and jetlag would've passed by now. I feel hungover and too tired to function the way I want to. I'm not assigned to any of the rigs today so Chief tells me that we're going to look for a nightstand for my bedroom.

I pull my hair into a low bun, get dressed in my khaki pants, tan combat boots, and fire department T-shirt, and head out to the apparatus bay. The large bay houses a fire engine, two aircraft-rescue trucks, and a heavy-duty rescue truck. The roof is high up so that the large vehicles can fit inside, and there are large, open garage doors in the front and the back of each vehicle. Because of the large, open space, there are tons of pigeons flying around under the roof and pigeon droppings all over the cement bay floor.

A dust storm rolled in last night. As I walk out the door to the apparatus bay, I'm surprised to be greeted by a thick, orange fog. I've never seen anything like this before. It's my first glance of the base during daylight and all I see is a dust storm. Even nearby objects are obscured by the orange haze.

Chief and I get into the battalion rig and he drives me through the base. My eyes are still heavy and my social skills are a little unavailable at the moment.

My head tracks from left to right out the passenger window as I take in the view of my new temporary home. *"What did I get myself into?"* I think. I begin to feel slightly depressed as I peer out at the desolate, arid, desert. We pass a long junkyard filled with old, broken-down military vehicles. Tankers after tankers are lined up, side by side and have been left abandoned. There are piles of rubbish everywhere and long stretches where there is no inhabitance.

I don't see anyone else around and we pull up to a U-shaped housing unit that looks like an abandoned motel from a horror film. Chief puts the Jeep in park and opens the car door that sounds like an empty tin can. I sit for a moment, confused as to what exactly the plan is. Finally, I get up off the sun-degraded, chipped seat cover and follow along.

We enter one of the rooms to see some dusty furniture, broken and tipped over. My mouth opens as an outward expression of my inner confusion. Chief sees a nightstand in the corner and inspects it carefully. There's no power to the building so there are no lights, but the rooms are small enough that the light from outside appropriately illuminates the whole area. At this point, I'm not feeling fearful that chief has drug me over here for ill intentions; I'm just dumbfounded by the simple fact that we're rummaging through an abandoned building for furniture right now. Chief has been here so long that he forgets how strange this whole thing must be for a newcomer.

He continues to pragmatically scavenge through the rooms while dusting off furniture and looking for some level of quality. Finally, he finds one he's proud of. He passes me the nightstand with a couple of pigeon droppings on top. "You can just clean that up when we get back," he says. I grab the filthy object, realizing that I'm here to get dirty and there's no reason to try to avoid it. I will quickly get used to starting my mornings sweaty and covered in Iraqi dirt, possibly with a side of pigeon pooh.

While sitting on my squeaky, twin-sized bed I can feel the building rattle from a nearby Blackhawk helicopter taking off. The vibrations come through our thin, white walls as readily as they would a paper Dixie cup.

Our station is right next to the airfield so Blackhawks and Chinooks are flying around us all day and night. For some reason, I take extra notice to the vibrations of this Blackhawk taking off when suddenly I hear a new sound.

Is that what I think it is? My eyes widen. I straighten my back in alert, like a meerkat sensing danger. Adrenaline pumps through my veins as I hear a loud siren and a big voice shouting, "Incoming! Incoming! Incoming!"

My heart thumps forcefully in my chest, as if it might jump out of my throat. I think of the only suitable reaction for this scenario. I need to get to the bunkers. There's an explosion! The blast pushes me off balance and the white walls around me thunder and shake like a loud earthquake. It felt like a mortar hit right next to us.

I duck down and exit my room, hustling to the bunkers. Everyone else has the same idea. A dozen firefighters simultaneously exit their bedrooms into one long, narrow hallway. Everyone is in crouched positions with expressions of focus and feet moving as quickly as they can. This scene couldn't be choreographed any better if it was planned—the sight of several large men all crunched down and mouse-like in their posture and footsteps. The thought that goes through everyone's mind in a matter of moments is "Do I move, or do I stay?"

We all make it to the bunker just outside the station and listen closely to our radios. A little bit of nervous laughter comes out as the relief sets in.

"That was a close one!" several exclaim.

The nervous chatter of adrenaline rushed junkies begins.

"Did you feel that?"
"That must've hit so close!"
"That was crazy!"

We continue to listen and wait for the all-clear sign from Base Defense.

"Hopefully, no one got hit," we all think as we continue to listen for radio traffic.

Luckily, no one is hurt and we aren't dispatched for any medical emergencies.

A rocket was launched onto our base and landed in the airfield next to us. Although we only felt one explosion, we are informed that several mortars were shot over our walls. The rest of them were UXO (unexploded ordinances) so the military will have to perform controlled detonations on them.

"All stations stand by for wake-up tones." The low and high tones go off, followed by the fire alarm.

"The time now is 0640 (6:40 a.m.). Twenty minutes until morning briefing," says the dispatcher over the intercom.

I'm finally getting into the groove of living at Taji Air Base Fire Station 1. The first two days at my base were stressful. I felt tired and depressed. I finally kicked the jetlag completely and feel on the appropriate schedule. My only hindrance to good sleep is my roommate that seems to inhabit my floor tiles at night and makes incessant chirping sounds that not even earplugs can block.

Finally, the guy in the room next to me got tired of the chirping as well. He found some "Off" bug spray and went on a cricket hunt in my room. We'll see if he chirps tonight.

While I was in Texas, I chose not to wear makeup; I only wore jeans and T-shirts. I am the solo woman of the group and not here to attract attention from my male counterparts. Although self-conscious at first, I was able to regain my confidence after a few days and accept the freshness and liberation of my natural self. I have zero intentions of finding a male companion exceeding the rank of friendship, and I plan to maintain that status throughout my tour in the Middle East.

Because of the close quarters we all live in here at Taji, it's especially imperative to maintain a strong stance of my intentions with the opposite sex. I enjoy the level of respect that I've gained by not swaying from my path. I know the dominant understanding is that I want to be a firefighter, and I'm traveling strong and solo to obtain this goal.

There are a lot of great people here. The first people who I became friends with were Robert and Ryan. Ryan is a west coaster too, but with his accent, I wouldn't have placed him in California. I'm guessing he's a transplant.

Some of the guys warned me about him. "Watch out for him." They pointed at him in the DFAC. "He's a prankster. Don't trust him."

The other guys joke with him about the California-boy look he sports with the platinum-blond, spiky hair and tanned skin. He's a good guy and always sports an "up to no good" look on his face. I can't help but laugh when I'm around him.

Robert has the same effect; the concoction of Robert and Ryan leads to nothing but trouble. They show no mercy against who they prey upon to formulate a good prank. I, on the other hand, am not a good prankster and kind of a chicken when it comes to firehouse pranks. Too many people have been hurt or sent home because of firehouse pranks gone awry. Besides, I lack the creativity in thinking of original gags.

Robert is a master at digital art and photography and likes to print out digitally enhanced photos, while adding captions and graphics to make someone else the butt of the joke. He hangs the photos on the walls and ceilings for all to see. Ryan is less technological in his approach. He will just walk up to a Ugandan guard at the DFAC and point at someone while saying, "They're trying to steal food. 'Don't let them leave the building." The guard will then stare at that person for a moment while clutching an AK-47, and then let out little laugh or an annoyed reaction when realizing he's joking.

Robert and Ryan treat me like a sister. Sometimes, we're all in cahoots, but sometimes, they'll just treat me like the little sister that needs to be made embarrassed, often.

After morning wake-up tones, Robert blares his music as we all clear our eyes and pull ourselves from our squeaky little beds.

Robert's room is on the corner where two hallways crisscross. One hallway is the entrance from the apparatus bay to the day room, and the other through the middle of the long dormitory area. You can't go outside without passing by. He turns up his music and stands out in the hallway singing and rapping to his songs with a pleased look on his face.

Robert is tall with blue eyes and light-blond hair. He dreams of being a pilot one day. He's at the point of almost completing his second year in Iraq.

And then there was my travel companion who I flew over with from Baghdad. Oh Lopez, you're so full of it sometimes. We were constantly giving each other a hard time when we crossed paths. Since we were at separate stations, we didn't cross paths as often. We had to ride backward in the same engine together for a week or two and the conversations were always comical to me. We found out that we were both divorced and he proceeded to find ways to try to make me feel bad about it.

"What was your wedding song?" he asked in his tough voice.

"I don't remember," I said back to him, not wanting to give him any ammunition. "What was *your* wedding song?" I competed.

Somehow, we got a hold of each other's wedding songs, and from that point on, we would tauntingly sing the other person's song to try to make the other feel bad. It was hilarious more than painful when we ended up in the day room of station 1 with one arm around the other singing each other's country song as obnoxiously as possible. I actually missed that character when his contract year was over and he left Taji. Luckily for me, I at least got some hand-me-downs: a blanket, a lamp, and a couple of other necessities. That's how we roll here at Taji; we scrounge for items from those who have moved out and we also go on the occasional abandoned building hunt.

And then there's my partner Javon, who I ride in the back of the engine with most of the time. He's a firefighter in Georgia with plans to return to work for the city department when he leaves Iraq. We have to spend so much time together in the back of that fire engine, in that heat, driving around and conducting inspections on the military housing units. Our partnership started out strong and then our relationship has changed dynamically as one minute we're diverting our bodies as far as possible, skin crawling to hear one another speak. The next moment, we're happy as can be, tipping our heads and swaying our bodies side to side while snapping our fingers to the beat of Kid Cudi's song "Why Are You So Paranoid?"

Another one of my good friends is Hugo. He speaks Spanish and lets me practice speaking to him since I'm trying to learn. Most of the time, I just call him Mocoso, which means "booger face," and he calls me the female version: Mocosa.

Hugo is an ex-marine, but still a marine at heart, and proud of it. He's one of the hardest workers we have at the station, and he'll be outside moving around fire extinguishers and cleaning up more than most others when it's over 120 degrees outside. His positive attitude is the epitome of what you would hope to discover from an honorable and proud service member of our nation. Sometimes, when the work is done, we'll have long and thoughtful conversations about life and the future while perched on top of fire extinguisher pallets—and those conversations are in English, of course.

In the rest of my free time, I have to admit that I talk to Alex. After our conversation back in Texas, he found me on Facebook. We have conversations every day now since the reconnection. I really think I like this guy. We've even progressed from typing on Skype to video chat. It's exciting because things seem to be progressing.

Every time I talk to Alex, I feel comforted by his voice. There's always a pressure when you're the only woman working in a group of men. I know I'm different from them, and I feel more pressure to be on top of my game. Although my coworkers have been great to me, I know that I can't let my guard down. With Alex, I feel like I can. He's very encouraging to me. Our conversations help ease the stress.

Fire Diary

Alex is a year younger than me and we were both previously married but have no children. Alex and I also have a lot of mutual friends. I live with five guys here who have lived and worked with him at other bases around Iraq, or in the air force, in Guam. They all speak highly of him and acknowledge that he is a good firefighter, and lieutenant. It seems like such a small world. There are three guys over at his base that I trained with during ARFF school in Texas.

I found out that Alex's dad passed away just weeks before I met him. His dad was sick one day, went to the hospital, and they told the family he had stage 4 lung cancer. They were shocked and unaware. He passed away just one week later. His dad wasn't a smoker; it was from years of work as a welder and pipe fitter. He had traveled the nation working on large projects in his occupation and acquired irreversible lung damage from inhalation of harsh particles. Alex admired his dad and misses him severely.

To be expected, the sudden death has left a gaping metaphorical wound on Alex's life. I collect that he has pain and confusion, but he tries to be strong. Alex talks a lot about his family. I sit back and admire him as he expresses his genuine love and care for his mother, his brother, and his two-year-old niece.

My chief told me that Alex was actually present during one of the firefighter deaths here in Iraq. It was Alex's friend and engine partner who was killed when the cigarette-lit rocket exploded in front of the firehouse. Alex was first on scene to his tragic end. Alex had never mentioned this to me. I wasn't sure if it was okay for me to bring it up. I finally ask him about the incident, and he gives me details on the accident. The engine crew just came back to the station after a round of building inspections. The crew was taking a quick break. Alex was sitting in the fire engine, waiting for his crew to return. One of the crewmembers was taking a cigarette break, just outside the apparatus bay, where Alex was waiting. Suddenly, Alex looked up and saw the firefighter running with a flaming rocket shell in his hands. When the rocket exploded, a large chunk of metal was shot backward in a trajectory toward Alex. Instead of flying through the fire engine and hitting him, the flying debris smashed into a concrete pillar right in front of him. Alex's life was almost lost that day as well.

After an early morning truck fire and a small rubbish fire, I again hear the radio traffic announcing, "Stand by for emergency traffic."

Dispatch continues. "Chief 1, Chief 2, Engine 1, Tanker 2, respond to a rubbish fire in the bone yard."

Javon and I hop in the back of the engine and don our bunker gear and SCBA. As we get closer to the bone yard, Captain spots the location of the fire. When riding backward in a fire engine, it's tough for you to see what the emergency or fire scene looks like, so you just have to trust your officer to guide you to do the right thing.

The fire engine idles on the pavement while Captain jumps out of his seat to grab the bolt cutters. Out the side window, I see him cutting a chain that is wrapped around a metal gate. Just to the left of the metal gate is a sign that says in red, "No Dumping," and in black underneath, "Of Any Trash in This Area." Behind this sign is a mile-long area filled up of the most spectacular rubbish I have ever seen.

"I want everyone masked up and on air," Captain demands.

I've never had to put my mask on and hook it up to my breathing apparatus while still in the fire engine before. Confused by this new tactic, I do as I'm told and don my face piece. As I plug my air tank into my mask, our engine driver slowly drives off the pavement and through the gate and rolls onto the sandy desert surface of Iraqi dirt.

We drive through the bone yard and I'm peering out the side window while my air tank causes my every breath to sound loud and dramatic.

This field is massive and consumed by an amazing collection of war memorabilia. The content of the bone yard is of high danger, including thousands of old military vehicles, every type you can think of from the Saddam regime. I see rockets and twenty-foot-long missiles lying on the ground. Large belts of machine gun rounds lie among the debris. The rounds look like they could be Rambo's necklace, but I believe they are fighter jet ammunition rounds. Crushed cars are on their side and tossed on top of destroyed Connex boxes. There are small, wrecked structures and more. This is a dumpsite for war accessories.

We arrive to a smoky, flaming pile of rubbish amid the heap of trash. I jump out of the fire engine with my partner and pull the hose line from the front bumper. I call to the engineer for water and our hose-line swells with pressure.

I open the nozzle and aim toward the fire while my partner stands behind me, holding the line for support.

The flames are knocked down quickly, so I shut down the nozzle to evaluate the situation. A puddle of water forms on top of the sand and remains deep, as it will not evaporate into the hardened earth of the desert.

A flame suddenly ignites from on top of the water. It flickers and glides along the surface. We freeze in our tracks and stand silent as we assess the strange fire behavior. Fire is not supposed to dance on top of water. Chief, Captain, my partner, and I stand motionless in trepidation of what is about to happen. Are we in danger here? We consider this thought as we try to understand what we're dealing with. This isn't magnesium because it would be volatile once in contact with water. Hopefully, it isn't dynamite and we're now staring at the lit end.

We finally extinguish the reigniting flames and conclude that it's some sort of nonmiscible fuel; this would explain the flame's ability to burn on the water surface. I'm glad we weren't caught in a dangerous situation here.

Our captain took caution to advise us to go "on air" (SCBA and mask hooked up) just prior to arrival to protect ourselves from harmful or carcinogenic products of combustion. Captain explained later that there's a lot of depleted uranium lying around in the bone yard and this is highly dangerous to be anywhere near.

After returning to quarters, I conduct an Internet search on depleted uranium. On my screen, I see horrid pictures of deformed babies from pregnant women who were exposed. It's used in some weapons and aircrafts and people can be exposed through inhalation and other methods. Exposure can have long-term health effects on kidneys and lungs due to radiological toxicity. Reading about the danger of this stuff makes me feel nervous of all the potential hazards.

Chapter 9
Groundhog Day

I LIVE WITH TWENTY GUYS IN this building. We have no real silverware. The only eating utensils that we possess are plastic sets that we take from the DFAC (dining facility). Each set has a spoon, knife, and fork in a little bag. Usually, the spoon and fork are taken from the set first, leaving a lazy mess of ripped plastic bags containing one plastic knife. You have to dig through the clutter to find if any good utensils remain. The only other kitchenware we have is one plastic bowl, which I'm not sure anyone actually washes.

I heat up a packet of instant oatmeal in the only ceramic mug that I possess and sit on my bed to eat it. I could only find a plastic knife this time, so I scrape the bottom of my mug and balance a glob of the undermoistened nutrients on the narrow, flimsy utensil.

We don't have an oven or stove. None of the living quarters here are supposed to have any sort of stovetop because of the significant fire hazard from bad electrical work and flimsy buildings. We have two microwaves and two refrigerators. One of our refrigerators is completely filled with one-liter water bottles, and one is filled with Styrofoam to-go boxes from the DFAC.

The water bottles here are abundant because it's the only water we can drink. Everywhere we go, there are pallets filled with hundreds of bottles of water. The water is drafted from some nasty lake in Baghdad. It's chemically treated so intensely that it's stripped of all minerals. We have to add electrolytes to the water bottles every now and then or we won't get hydrated properly due to the lack of minerals. I heard a rumor that you could sit in a bath full of this water, throw in something electrical, and not get killed because there's no mineral for the electrical current to conduct. Well, I won't be experimenting with that one.

In Iraq, every day seems like the rest; the days blur together. We work, we eat at the DFAC, and we go to the gym. Exercising is so important in this environment. When living, working, and eating with the same people every single day, we need the stress outlet that exercise can provide to relieve tensions and monotony. My engine crew and I head out to the gym around the same time every day.

There's very little to do to break the Groundhog's Day effect around here. Browsing the PX (post exchange) to buy treats or magazines is one of the few things to do, other than working out. Our PX is a little grocery store, lightly stocked with necessities and some extra items. If something that we want or need is not on the shelf, we will have to patiently wait a few days for the shipment to come in from a convoy. If I know I'm gonna need deodorant or a hygienic item, I buy it while it's on the shelf, and before I need it.

I arrive to the PX today with a craving for chocolate, knowing that I may not get what I desire. Chocolate doesn't come in too often because it doesn't travel well in 115 degree (or higher) temperatures. When chocolate treats do come in, they metaphorically fly off the shelf from anxious customers awaiting the suppressant of their cravings.

It's my lucky day and I find a Twix bar. I smile inside as I take my indulgence from the shelf, knowing that it's now solidified in the package only after being in a previously melted condition. I can predict that the caramel is probably hardened now from reconstituting itself in the cool, air-conditioned environment of the PX and no longer ooey-gooey like I want it to be. It will probably stick in my teeth and drive me nuts, but I'm gonna love it anyways.

I wait in the checkout line behind a few soldiers with shopping baskets on the crook of their arms, filled with their own form of satisfactions: car magazines, Swedish Fish, peanut butter, and a jar of jelly. The three Pakistani cashiers are ringing up the customer's purchases as I patiently await my turn while looking at the shelf full of teddy bears that say, "Love from Iraq," and ceramic mugs that boast, "Iraq, Been There, Done That!" I've already bought my share of these souvenirs, but I still enjoy looking at them.

I always seem to arrive at the same cashier every time. I think he sees me in line and takes longer or shorter with his customers in order to time out my arrival to the front of line. Although I don't know this man's name, I appreciate the occasional and brief interaction with him. He asks me questions sometimes and tells me that he's from Pakistan but doesn't really have any family to go home to.

I didn't see the man at the PX for a while and I wondered why. One of the engine crews was called out to a car fire the other day and arrived on scene to a cold, soot-covered car that had burned up overnight. There was a body in the car of a man who didn't make it out alive. It was reportedly the body of a Pakistani man. I was worried it might by my friend since he was absent from the PX. A week later, I saw him back at work and I was thankful he was still alive.

Since our base is like a small community, I enjoy the brief interactions with random acquaintances. It's also nice to interact with other people around that you don't have to live with and see on an hourly basis.

There are many men and women from Uganda working as guards, but a few of the more charismatic individuals have become friends in passing. Their ability to understand English is minimal, but their smiling faces are wonderful to see. We greet by saying, "Jumbo," which means "What's up?" in Swahili.

I also have a friend from Turkey; His name is John. He sells beautiful Arabic decanters and wine glasses at the bazaar next to the PX. I met John one day while he was looking for medicine at the PX. He was feeling sick and asked for my advice on what to buy. He told me that his throat felt tight during the sand storms and they aren't allowed to see the doctor here. They have to go home to Turkey to see one.

John and I briefly chat when we bump into each other on the base. Today he saw my firefighter brothers and was looking for me. "Where is the desert princess?" he asks. I thought that was a sweet yet undeserving reference, but I'll take it! (Smiles.)

It seems like no matter how hard I try, I can't avoid letting the truth out that I'm a huge klutz.

It's lunch and time to go through the thrice daily routine. The Ugandan guard checks my ID, I proceed to the washroom to clean my hands, scan my ID, and grab my plastic silverware, plastic plate, and brown cafeteria-style lunch tray. I receive the standard delightful smiles from the little Indian men who stand behind steamy, hot silver containers with a scoop in hand. They're always hopeful and encouraging of me to have some of the food that they are serving in the buffet line. Whether it's beans, cornbread, veggies, or fried food, I almost feel bad declining their invitation to hand over my plate and let them fill it up. This is what they do every single day, three times a day, so you can't really blame them for their ease in excitement.

Today I accept an invitation to hand over my flimsy white picnic-style plate with its divided ridges that allocate a spot for a main course and two small sides. I hand it to the kind Indian man and say, "Spaghetti, please!"

With a pleased smile, the small man loads the main section of my picnic plate with spaghetti noodles and meat sauce. I smile back at him confidently.

Forgetting about the simple construction of my picnic-style plate, I proceed to grab the plate from the empty side. I then watch in slow-motion horror as my flimsy plate bends downward from the weight of spaghetti and plops down onto the glass of the buffet line. Red meat sauce and noodles slide down the glass, leaving a red streak as it easily negotiates its way down into a big, sloppy pile on the floor in front of me. If real life had background music, I would now be hearing the sound of the instruments played in a horror scene.

The line of military men and women behind me comes to a halt and all I can do is stand in my embarrassment while my engine partner, Ryan, points and laughs at me. Thanks, Ryan.

A nice army woman steps in next to me to break my frozen-in-the-headlights moment by directing me on my next course of actions. She so sweetly takes my awkwardness into her own hands and requests that one of the men help me by grabbing a mop bucket.

"Thank you," I say to her shyly.

My engine crew continues to have a great time laughing it up. For some reason though, I can laugh at myself way more than anyone else can. By the time they're done laughing, I'm still trying really hard not to bust out into spontaneous laughter while replaying my embarrassing moments. My crew said the best part is I gave up on the spaghetti and walked to the other side of the DFAC to make a sandwich instead.

Sooo bored! Before I got here, I remember people talking about Groundhog Day. Every day is the same. I'm definitely feeling and understanding the full meaning of Groundhog Day in Iraq. It's been four months since I've worn normal street clothes, had a day off work, eaten with non-plastic utensils on a non-plastic plate, and seen a child or non-pigeon animal.

Every week is the same: we conduct inspections on buildings, fill out paperwork, teach fire extinguisher classes to the military and TCN, and run structure fire or airfield drills. We also have an occasional EMS, fire, or airfield call.

Occasionally, we go through the building and collect all our personal documents that need to be thrown away. If it has family names and addresses or other personal or security information, we have to burn it in the burn barrel. We don't want our security to be compromised if this information makes it into the wrong hands.

Today, in all our boredom, Lieutenant Norm and I decide to play a game of burn-barrel baseball. It's one hundred twenty degrees Fahrenheit outside and we're pitching wadded paper at each other over a fiery barrel in the heat of the day. Norm and I stand on each side of the flaming barrel. He wads up a document and pitches it over the flames. I take a stick and swing, trying to hit the paper ball into the barrel. We laugh at ourselves, knowing how silly this is, but it's just another idea to keep from the monotony.

Norm and I work together most days. We enter data from building inspections into the computer and take turns giving fire safety and extinguisher presentations. He's been a great friend as well and has helped me adapt to all my extra duties at the firehouse.

After everyone's individual tasks are achieved, we often find ourselves going stir crazy from the Groundhog Day effect.

Everyone at the firehouse has his or her own form of entertainment to combat the bland environment. Some of us get really excited about the aircrafts that fly in. On occasion, we hear loud thundering sounds along with the sound of large engines slowing down a powerful piece of machinery; we run outside and try to spot the big aircraft flying in for a landing. "Did you see that plane?" we exclaim. "It was huge! I think it's a C5. No, maybe a C17." We try to identify the types of aircraft. It reminds me of little kids telling "big fish" stories.

Living right next to the flight line has its advantages and disadvantages. The advantage is being able to sit outside and watch the Blackhawks hover just above the ground, for several minutes at a time. I've fallen in love with Chinooks and Blackhawks from being able to gaze at them in all their majesty. The disadvantage is the constant sound of propellers at all hours. I've grown used to the sound of them, and I'm able to sleep through it. I'm also now able to sleep through the sound of mortars from afar. I don't always know if I'm hearing a car bomb or IDF (indirect fire), but the pressure from the explosion makes a closed door slam. I hear them at night on occasion. Whoomp, whoomp, whoomp! I acknowledge the sounds of the explosions and then fall back to sleep with surprising ease.

I'm having a hard day. It's Groundhog Day. Not really, but the monotony and the feeling of being caged has set in. Every day is the same; I have to look up the date to actually put it on my daily entry. I rarely even know what day of the week it is and I'm feeling highly irritated with everyone around me. It's so hot outside that our rigs keep breaking down and I feel like I can't work out, eat, or go to the PX when I want to. Okay, I guess I'm done complaining.

Other than my moments of boredom, I haven't been homesick. I get to speak to my family on Skype every week. It's comforting to hear their voices and see their blurry faces behind the subpar network connection. Despite the connection barriers, it's amazing that I can actually see my family from halfway around the world.

I really have adapted to the environment and only sustain short inconveniences of displeasure. When I do begin to think about home, I find it strange what I miss the most. I miss being out in the forest. I changed the wallpaper on my laptop to a picture that epitomizes the serenity of my passion for the outdoors. A moss-covered footpath cut through a lush temperate rainforest with tall trees in every direction and ground covering of bright green clovers and ferns. *This is where I would like to be,* I think. Just like hunting season, I would be there—just me and my compound bow-and-arrows with alternating zebra-stripe and neon-pink fletching.

Maybe I miss the forest so much because it's a place of stillness and natural beauty. It's a place where you can clear your mind of the clutter and chaos of life and just breathe fresh air.

Chapter 10
Military/Iraq Updates

"The time now is 0644 ... Morning briefing in twent—sixteen minutes." This morning's dispatch is a little thrown off by our abnormal morning incident.

Over an Hour Earlier ...

It's 0500 (5:00 a.m.) and I'm awoken by the dispatcher's voice in the hallway speakers. "Chief 1 and Chief 2 stand by for unknown emergency."

Although I'm not Chief 1 or 2, I decide it would behoove me to get up quickly so I can at least put a sports bra on under my shirt. I also put on my tall socks, because I absolutely hate putting on my bunker boots with short socks on or—worse—no socks.

Radio traffic halts and still no tones are activated. I get up and use the latrine. I don't feel alarmed or hurried at this point. I just want to make sure I'm ready if something happens.

A location of this unknown emergency is given so I proceed to the engine and jump in my bunker gear. Luckily, I choose to do so because there's a request for engine crews from both stations. I still don't know the level of urgency, but I will be as prepared as I need to be.

SCBA (self-contained breathing apparatus) or no SCBA? Well, I don't know what kind of emergency we're responding to. Comms (communications) aren't working well on base so I don't know if we're going to a fire, a hazmat (hazardous-material) scene, or a medical call. Whatever the emergency is, we quickly begin to sense from dispatch that this is something troubling.

While riding to the location, lights and sirens on, dispatch attempts to verbalize updated information but all we hear is "SSshhkwwksh."

We arrive on scene and hear Chief 1's radio traffic. "Bring the engine! Bring the medics! Bring *everyone!*"

I jump out of the rig and hear, "He's not breathing!"

I grab the AED (automated external defibrillator) and my partner grabs the medical bag. We dash over to a metal, hydraulic radar tower located twenty yards away.

Inside is a young military man lying unconscious and pulseless. There are a dozen of our firefighters on scene now. We pull the man down out of the metal tower and find that a shock is advised by the AED.

We all stand back while the AED powers up and prepares the delivery of a high electrical charge. The machine powers up and prompts us to push the button to deliver a shock. The button is pushed and an electrical charge shocks directly to the soldier's heart, causing his body to jump off the ground. A second shock is advised. The machine makes a loud sound as it charges up to deliver the second voltage.

We are now surrounded by soldiers looking on at the devastating event. The distraught faces of soldiers, friends, and coworkers of this man are standing or kneeling down, but all are standing back and watching with grief as we continue CPR and do our best to circulate oxygenated blood through this man's body.

The sun is rising up beyond and I see the new day shining up over a dusty mound casting long shadows from the men in uniform standing by. This isn't the way we expect to start a new day. It almost seems insulting to see the sun shine so brightly and new at this very moment. I see one of the kneeling soldiers in his combat boots, camo pants, and tan T-shirt; he rubs his thumb and forefinger across his eyes with his head down. My heart hurts for these men.

With two shocks on board, we coordinate our CPR with thirty chest compressions to two breaths via bag-valve mask and high-flow oxygen at twenty-five liters per minute. After I take my turn on chest compressions, the medics take over care of our patient. We load him into the back of the ambulance. He will have to take life flight to Balad Air Base.

The story we receive during patient care is that he was pinned in the pinch-point of a hydraulically assisted door, which squished his chest. It sounds as if the metal door was closing and he saved someone's life by pushing them out of the way, causing him to be pinched between the strong hydraulic forces.

Later, we get word that the young man lived for a day at the military hospital, but his body couldn't recover from the trauma and he passed away. My prayers go out to his family.

This week is the start of the Muslim holy month of Ramadan. Muslims don't eat or even drink water, from sun up until sun down. There's speculation of an increase in IDF during this time because, for some reason, there's an increase of these events on most holidays. We don't always know what's going on outside the wire. Being that we're civilians, we don't always get updates on some of the attacks. The daily newspaper *Stars and Stripes* (the Middle East edition) is a good source to keep us informed on what actually is going on out there. There are still hundreds of innocent people being killed: Iraqis, Americans, and anyone else in the way of their religious agenda.

I work a short day today since I'm not assigned to the engine. My task for the day is to destroy fifty fire extinguishers. I start these tasks early because it's a laborious job that I prefer not to do in the afternoon heat.

All the nitrogen needs to be expelled from the extinguisher first, and then clamps and wrenches are used to physically dismantle the tops of them. We pour the remaining powder into large, blue, hazmat containers, and then we drill a hole into two sides of the metal canister. I was told the hole is to keep insurgents from utilizing these containers as improvised explosive devices.

Many of the fire extinguishers here are not up to code and may even be hazardous to use on a fire; that's why we destroy them completely.

By the end of my destruction duties, I'm filthy, covered in yellow and purple dry chem. I jump in the shower and clean up.

There's a new guy at our station, so I'm given permission to take the utility truck and give him a tour of the base. He and I bring our cameras along so we can take pictures of the old buildings.

Mortared and crumbled structures stand abandoned. Remnants of homes are riddled with bullet holes and broken glass. Many still expose the pride that was once held upon them with paintings and abstract design on the clay exterior. Palm trees and white bricks ornament the dirt yards.

We step out of the truck to explore some of the degraded buildings. Some don't even have doors because there was no purpose or hope for return. Arabic writing is painted on the side of this house and we take pictures of each other in front of it.

While taking pictures, I hear sirens across the wire. We're only a quarter mile from the outside of the base where the freeway and city of Taji are located. The sirens only last a short time and are followed by the sound of automatic weapon fire. No sounds follow.

That was the second time I've heard automatic weapon fire over the wire. We won't find out what caused it, so there's no point in being too curious.

We hop back in the truck and drive toward the structure we're most curious about. A large building and property are surrounded by yellow caution tape. Signs are located on the property stating that no one is to step past the barricades. We don't really want to come any closer anyways; this is the "Chemical Ali building." The notorious cousin of Saddam Hussein was known for mixing deadly chemicals to commit genocide to other tribes, specifically the Kurdish people. Unfortunately, he was successful in killing many thousands. This building is condemned from all the dangerous substances that were and remain present.

I only have two friends on this base that are women: Janisse and Vanessa. Both of them are in the army and work as interrogators. Their official job title is human intelligence collector. Because of the security risk and interaction with locals, they don't wear ranks on their uniforms. Instead of a patch over the sternum with their rank, they have a patch that says, "US." Their identity is also protected by replacing the badge of their last name with a fake name. They were both given beautiful Persian names to represent their identities: Leila and Yasmine.

I met Janisse and Vanessa at the gym. Our engine crew worked out at the same time as them almost every day. My crew was already acquainted with them and would talk to them all the time. The girls wouldn't even acknowledge me at first. They were more difficult to win over than the men in my firehouse. Both are beautiful, proud, hardworking women and I admired them from the start—even though I would smile in their direction and was lucky if they looked in mine. I understood that as a civilian woman working on their military base, I needed to earn their trust. After a while, they grew to appreciate my focus and work ethic from the small encounters. Finally, they opened up to me and began to enjoy my presence as much, if not more, than the guys. It's wonderful to have friends here now who aren't guys.

Janisse is a wife and mother of four. She always has her dark hair pinned back in the most perfect bun I've ever seen. She must have really long hair, but I would never know because of the professional look she secures. She also amazes me with the amount of weight she can lift at the gym. I underestimated her slender figure and am continuously surprised by her strength and desire to challenge herself.

Vanessa is a young single woman who isn't afraid to tell the boys when they're out of line. I admire the way she speaks out to them when they come on to her too strong. She's a stand-up, God-fearing woman who shows honor to her military service.

Janisse and Vanessa meet with Iraqi citizens regularly because of their special job duties. They mentioned to me that sometimes the Iraqis would bring them homemade meals and insisted I try it sometime. For the amount of US citizens currently living in Iraq, it doesn't seem there are very many who have the opportunity to try real homemade Iraqi cuisine. Concurrently, there are probably not many who feel trusting enough to place food in their mouth that has been brought in from outside "the wire."

After my workout, Janisse and Vanessa hand me a large plate with a full leg of lamb resting on a bed of jasmine rice, garnished with yellow raisins and almonds. "One of the Iraqi ladies made this for us," Janisse says.

I take the dish back to the firehouse and put it in the fridge. Later, I pull it out to see if anyone else wants to try the lamb and rice. There's plenty of food and I offer it to some of the guys passing by the day room.

"No way," one of them says.

I'm excited to try it, so it doesn't bother me that no one will take me up on the opportunity to share a cultural experience. I have enough food for the next two days. It's delicious.

I had a bad dream last night. I dreamed that our perimeters were breached by insurgents and we were hiding in one of the abandoned buildings on base. They found us and started dropping poisonous chemicals into the building. I was trying to hold my breath and I started to "skip-breath," which is a firefighter technique of preserving remaining air when wearing an SCBA. After a while, I woke myself up because I really was holding my breath. I was still in a light sleep and I was skip-breathing.

I had to tell myself, "It's okay, Lizzy. It was just a dream." I began to breathe normal again and went back to sleep. But for a moment, I was feeling fear.

This was only the second time I felt afraid. The first time was when I had the dream on the plane a few months ago about being bombed. I guess I'm feeling a little bit unsure about the upcoming months when the president pulls out the majority of the soldiers. Our base is getting downsized by half, while the other half is being handed back to the Iraqis. Some of the little businesses are closing down and many of the TCN are leaving too. This base will be completely different in one to two months, and I could even get transferred to another base at any time.

The last of the American "combat troops" have pulled out of Iraq. The amount of remaining military personnel is slim, and although they aren't considered combat troops, we all know that the missions from Operation Iraqi Freedom can't just end without transitions. The name of the mission is now Operation New Dawn, and as usual, the name change and job title transitions don't necessarily mean things are different. Although it's a positive transition, there's uncertainty as to how well things will go over. Will the remaining soldiers be at higher risk, or is it stable enough for this transition to be seamless?

We're informed that our personnel are on call as back up for the hospital. The pullout of troops has left the army hospital short-handed. If a mass casualty incident occurs, they will need all hands on deck. Because of this, we're running a lot of mass casualty drills and working side by side with the military to make sure we're coordinating well together.

Our engine crew exits the DFAC after dinner. We're all in a great mood. All our work is done and dinner was satisfying. It's the end of summer and we're used to being in the heat.

I swing my arms around playfully. "It feels awesome out here, not as hot as usual."

Ryan agrees. "Yeah, it does. I wonder what the temperature is."

"It's probably one hundred degrees, but it feels good to us," Captain says as he laughs.

Ryan drives us back to the station and we hop out of the engine to look at the thermostat.

"A hundred nine degrees!" Captain exclaims.

We congregate in the app bay with the other crew, laughing about our enjoyment of 109 degrees. Mid laugh, I look across the gravel road and see a line of soldiers outfitted in heavy artillery and Kevlar. I stop laughing out of respect of the platoon marching single file toward us, and I feel a sense of guilt. They pass us as they walk through our apparatus bay. Nods are exchanged from both sides and small smiles are produced, as if they want to show positive acknowledgment but a full smile may mentally distract them for their mission ahead. They continue in their heavy gear toward the entry control point (ECP) and head out to cross the wire on a mission.

Chapter 11
Almost Vacation Time!

I'M SO EXCITED! I'M GETTING my R&R (rest and relaxation) vacation planned out. In late October, I'll fly to Baghdad then Dubai then arrive in Dublin, Ireland. I'll spend two weeks solo while adventuring around Europe and then end my vacation in Rome.

Before I left Washington, I bought a fat travel book on Europe. I was invigorated every time I picked up that book and read about all the different countries I could see. There was a colorful map of the countries on the front page and I would study it for a long time, memorizing the location of the countries in relation to one another. I plan to visit three countries during my R&R, but it's difficult choosing which ones to visit. Ireland, Germany, Italy, Greece … I want to see them all. I figured I would be traveling by myself unless I got lucky and found someone who was as ambitious to travel as me, and someone that I could actually stand to spend that much time with. Surprisingly, most of the guys that are firefighters over here go back to the United States during their vacations, even the young single ones without children. The opportunity to travel couldn't be any better and I can't imagine just going home. The time difference from my home to Iraq is eleven hours and the jetlag alone is a displeasing proposition to me.

My buddy Ziggy is the only guy I know that traveled to Europe on his R&R. Ziggy told me how awesome Amsterdam and Germany were and he described his train ride through the Swiss Alps on his way to Italy. As soon as Ziggy mentioned the Swiss Alps, I realized I hadn't even considered going to Switzerland. I did some Google searches on Switzerland and definitively chose that as one of my destinations. I found a small village near the Matterhorn and thought that would be perfect. My itinerary has been solidified and I've booked my tickets to Ireland, Switzerland, and Italy.

I need to learn some basic German and Italian phrases for my travels to Switzerland and Italy. Different language is the common language in Switzerland. Because it's surrounded by Austria, Germany, Italy, and France, there are many languages spoken. I think some Deutsch (German) might be helpful. German is the dominant language in Zermatt, where I've chosen to venture.

Alex and I are still talking every day on Skype and Facebook. I like the connection because I feel it's a way we can communicate and learn about each other without being physical. We see each other on Skype and chat every morning and night. Over the few months that we've been talking, we've formed a relationship and have gone as far as discussing the possibility of marriage and children after we leave Iraq. Based on a nonphysical, personality, and character profile alone, we're crazy about each other. I'm kind of embarrassed to admit that. I've met him once in person and now we have a whole Internet relationship.

I tell Alex all about my itinerary. He mentions that his R&R is around the same time and he wants to meet up with me in Europe. He has to make arrangements to his current schedule and plane tickets in order to make this work.

Alex gets to work rearranging his vacation schedule and contacting the right people. Because of his vacation schedule, he's able to travel with me to Switzerland and Italy, but I'll be alone at my first destination to Ireland. He even wants to change his ticket so that we can fly out of Rome together and then part ways in London. I'll be heading back to the desert, and he'll be heading back to Texas for another week.

Alarms echo across base as bulletproof vests and Kevlar helmets are donned by all our crews. I climb in the back of the fire engine and glance at my partner as he struggles to get his helmet strap fastened.

Radio traffic from base defense states that there's been a mass casualty incident (MCI) outside of B-Pod (a housing area) and there are five victims suffering from shrapnel wounds.

Ryan drives the engine down the narrow clay-colored streets of Taji with lights and sirens. Military personnel peer through their weapons on rooftops in sniper position.

All apparatus arrive at B-Pod to find five Ugandan guards lying in a dusty parking lot. Some of the army personnel are out with the victims and preparing for triage. We jump out of the engine with every piece of medical equipment on board and Chief assigns my partner and me to a patient.

I kneel down next to the man and assess his situation. "What's wrong?" I ask.

The man looks at me, trying to hold back a smile. I realize he doesn't speak enough English to communicate with me so my partner so I flag down the army private nearest us. "What's supposed to be wrong with him?"

The army private kneels down to our level. "I think he's supposed to have shrapnel and profuse bleeding from his arm."

"Okay, thank you."

Good thing this is only a simulation drill. We take out our gauze and bandages and simulate that we're providing first aid for his wounds. I think it's actually more difficult to treat pretend wounds than real ones.

We triage our patient with a green tag and classify him as "walking wounded," but he still needs to be transported to the hospital for further care. We don't have all the medical supplies and transport units like back home so it's imperative we be resourceful. Our patient is guided to the bed of a little, white pickup truck, and a patient strapped to a backboard is loaded up next to him. One of our firefighters climbs in back to stabilize the backboarded man, and keep him from sliding around, while they drive to the hospital.

You would never put a backboarded patient in the bed of a pickup truck back in the United States, but things are different here. If mortars are coming over the walls, we need to strap up the patients and get everyone to safety ASAP. Next, the army medical staff will continue the simulation drill by providing further care for the patients.

Heading back to quarters, Ryan drives the engine down the road that parallels with the highway off base—outside the wire. A bus full of Iraqi workers exits the base to the main road. The barricade between base and the Iraqi side is lower right here and we're now driving parallel to the Iraqi workers that just egressed. My partner and I look over at the bus just in time to see one of the men flipping us his middle finger. Wow! I've seen on the news and in other forms of media the hatred that some Iraqis have for Americans, but this is the first time I've seen it directly here. I don't know why I'm surprised about this, but I am. He doesn't even know us, but if we're a part of a group that he hates, it doesn't matter who we are as individuals. I haven't seen this blatant dislike from any other Iraqis I've crossed paths with.

Just before dinner, we're toned out for a medical call at the convoy transient center where an Iraqi truck driver is having a syncopal episode (fainting).

Engine 1, engine 2, and both chiefs arrive to the scene. A large Iraqi man is up in the cab of his truck being assisted by two slimmer Iraqi men. I grab the medical bag from the engine and proceed toward the truck.

I climb up three ladder-like steps to enter the cab of the Mercedes-Benz commercial truck. The three men look at me astonished—I imagine from seeing a blonde American woman suddenly appearing in front of them. Their reaction startles me momentarily as I pause to assess the situation. After only a fraction of a moment, I'm able to decipher that my presence is accepted, just unexpected.

I begin to ask my typical patient questions and quickly realize there's a language barrier between us. The large man appears to be sick and not able to respond much. The two slim men are on each side of him, propping him up. These two men seem confused by my questions yet intrigued to have a conversation with me. One of the men speaks a little English and is able to answer some questions upon several attempts to rephrase my questions. We learn that the man is having severe right flank pain.

The two slim men and I slowly assist the larger man safely out of the cab and down to the dusty earth. The other firefighters greet us at ground level since there was no more room for people up in the cab. Then we all stand around, waiting for the medic unit to arrive. We only have fire engines and are not transport capable.

One of the Iraqi men looks at our group of firefighters and asks, "None of you speak Arabic?"

"No," we reply.

His face appears irritated and disappointed that we aren't able to speak their language.

I take another long look at our patient and think he looks a lot like Saddam Hussein. As I look at his paperwork, I notice at the end of his long four names is "Hussein."

The medics arrive and load him up after I receive a few more answers to our questions.

I realize that Hussein is a common last name. Although probably unlikely that this man is a brother or relative to Saddam, I remember hearing stories of one of his exiled brothers working at a barbershop at D9. D9 is a base where supposedly Delta Forces and other special forces were located. The location was supposed to be a secret, but last I heard, it was shut down. Although I'm in Iraq, I don't see how it's much of a secret if I know about it.

Saddam exiled some of his family members who didn't follow him. This supposed barbershop brother was exiled prior to operation Iraqi Freedom and that's why he wasn't in connection with the "wrong side." So the story goes.

I think it would be kinda cool if I just gave patient care to a relative of an infamous tyrant.

I've been wearing the same five pairs of khaki-cargo pants for almost five months now. Since I'm out in the heat so much, I only wear each pair once before I wash them, which has worn the material down. I was jumping out of the engine today when my pants pocket hung up on the door and I heard a dramatic tearing sound. I quickly covered my backside with a hand, not knowing how much of me was exposed. A three-inch hole tore through the weakened fabric in an L shape.

Now I've managed to hunt down a needle and green thread to stitch it up. The thread totally doesn't match, and my seamstress skills are horrible. Oh well. This saves me from having fewer khakis in the rotation.

The good news is I saw my first non-lizard, non-pigeon animal today. There was a really cute cat sprawled out near the PX. A couple of soldiers were standing around admiring it; they seemed overly excited about it as well. I haven't seen a cat since I was in Dubai.

Chapter 12
Baghdad/Dubai/Europe

IT'S CLOSE TO THE DAY I've always dreamed of. The day I would get to travel to Europe. It's been a lifelong dream of mine and I'm so close to finally fulfilling it. I can hardly wait!

Today I have a lot of paperwork to take care of before my travels; I have to pack and prepare my battle raddle (bulletproof vest and Kevlar helmet) for the helicopter flight over Baghdad. I'm packing very lightly, with one backpack of basic commodities, and I hope to purchase another backpack and a few more clothing items in Dubai. I have nothing that is weather appropriate for the fall or winter climates that I will be entering. There will be snow in Switzerland, and rain everywhere else.

My Taji brother, whose name is Fudge, will be traveling with me through Baghdad and Dubai. Fudge stands at six feet three inches tall, and he tells me that he's not only the youngest of his six sisters and three brothers, but he's also the shortest of them all. I laugh when I learn this information about him. He's like a big teddy bear, and I can't picture him being the youngest and smallest of such a large family. I've never heard the name Fudge before, but he says he's named after his grandpa Fudge. Fudge has been at Taji for a year now, has finished his contract, and is heading back home to Mississippi.

I'm thankful to have a travel companion, as I'm very afraid of being alone in the Middle East as a blonde American woman. I express my fears to Lieutenant Norman and Chief Menendez about getting abducted. "You have to come find me if I go missing," I state in a joking demeanor, with a definite serious undertone.

Fudge and I are ready to head out to Baghdad for the next couple of days, and I'm excited because Alex is going to be flying into Baghdad early to come see me.

We take flight by Chinook during the morning hours, and I'm soaking up the moment as I peer over the aerial view of Iraq during daytime. My first flight over was during the nighttime and I didn't get to see all of the terrain below. I'm thrilled to be flying over the Euphrates and Tigris rivers because I know these are landmarks of significant history and prophecy.

Once we arrive in Baghdad, we do more running around and signing in. They make sure we sign in every day for accountability. I'm happy to be back in Baghdad and able to say hi to many of the people I've met along the way.

I visit the firehouse next to the DFAC and sit down with my friends for a game of Wii. It's great to reconnect with them. To my surprise, my buddy Matt from Washington is now living here and working at this station. The last time I saw him was at his fire station in Washington. That's where I first heard he was traveling over here. It's not very often in Baghdad you run into an old fire friend from home. We were able to shoot the breeze and even chat about close friends, such as our good friend Gabe, who took care of me after my twenty-eighth birthday catastrophe.

Later in the Evening, Fudge and I catch a bus ride to another firehouse located near the on-base Iraqi prison. He knew several of the guys at this firehouse, but I knew none of them. I enjoy the opportunity to get a tour of another firehouse and see their fire engines.

Alex is here! He was able to pull some strings and leave his base early. The only problem is I'm heading to Ireland in two days, and now he has to wait in Baghdad until we meet in Switzerland. Oh well, I'm so happy he's here!

Last time I was in Baghdad, we stayed in close proximity to our sleeping quarters. I didn't know this base was so large. I'm getting to see more of Baghdad this time and learning more about the history behind the area. They actually have restaurants, which seems like a strange commodity over here. We have a little food court at our base, and I thought that was a big deal.

Alex and I catch a ride over to a Turkish restaurant. The interior is expansive and there are large groups of people eating together and celebrating a birthday. The atmosphere here is nothing like Taji. I almost feel like I'm back in the States because the civilians are dressed in their normal clothes and all hanging out like they're just regular, long-time coworkers. Well, I guess they probably are. A lot of people have worked here for the last five, six years.

Our waitress is from Lebanon, and we're at a Turkish restaurant, but we're ordering Indian food and a Greek appetizer. What a cultural combination! I'm just excited that we actually get to eat with real silverware on real plates. When you've eaten with plastic utensils for five months, the metal feels strange, yet fancy. The simplest pleasures stand out.

Alex and I are being really shy toward one another. I'm usually outgoing and easy to chat with, but we're just awkward now that we're together. I'm sure we'll warm up to each other and be able to act like our normal selves.

This morning I woke up at 0330 (3:30 a.m.) and got on the bus headed to BIAP (Baghdad International Airport). When Fudge and I arrived at the airport, we both noticed I was getting a lot of intense looks from the locals. I jokingly told him I needed him to be my bodyguard. He agreed to fulfill the duty.

While waiting in line at our terminal, I decide to use the public restroom. I enter the ladies room and am instantly reminded that they don't use toilet paper over here. I have no choice; I can't hold it. I sit down and look at the little hose that you're supposed to use to spray water on your underside. It looks filthy. *I am not about to touch that thing,* I think. I guess I have to go without toilet paper.

I exit the ladies room and a random stranger from the long line of contractors hollers out at me. "No toilet paper, huh?" Everyone laughs.

Luckily, I have a good sense of humor; otherwise, this could've been an embarrassing moment. We all laugh at my expense. No wonder no one else is going.

Our flight from BIAP to Dubai is about two hours. Fudge and I pick a row near the front and we sit in the cracks between the three seats to make it look like the whole row is taken. We're not in the mood to be squished, and there aren't assigned seats on this flight. It's a free-for-all.

The flight takes off and we have successfully hogged a whole row to ourselves on a fairly full flight. I suppose this may have been a little immature, but hey, sometimes it's totally worth it. More space for us.

This is a Jordan airline, and all the flight attendants are from Jordan. One of the male flight attendants keeps taking every opportunity to lean over Fudge and ask me if there's anything I need. Fudge's dimples get even deeper as he chuckles at me and shakes his head. Once more, the tall Jordanian man leans over Fudge and says to me, "Come. Join us in the back."

I know, I know. You're not supposed to go anywhere with strangers, but c'mon. This is an airplane. I'm a vigilant traveler and just enough paranoid, but I think I'm in a safe situation. I'm intrigued so I get up and walk toward the back rows to join the flight attendants: five males and one female.

The tall man introduces me to everyone. Two of them speak English, two sort of speak English, and two of them speak and understand zero English. They bring me a meal with lamb, pasta, and cheese while they talk to me about the war and enquire about our work. The man who invited me to the back used to be a translator for the US Army in the first years of the war. He went out on missions with them. His head hangs lower as he speaks of all the deaths he had to see and all the bombings he was lucky to escape from. He says he's glad he doesn't have to do that anymore.

The flight lands and we exit the plane. I meet back up with the rest of our crew and Fudge jokes about needing a raise as my bodyguard.

All the contractors are bussed to the Star Metro hotel. En route, we're briefed on the local religious laws and customs and told what to do if we are arrested in Dubai. We check into our rooms and clean up before heading to town for food.

Our original goal for the day was to find a camel and ski in the indoor skiing area at the mall. Neither of those things will probably happen because we've found ourselves busy shopping at the Mall of the Emirates. This is where the indoor skiing is located, but shopping is higher on the agenda. My shopping list consists of warm clothes for Europe. I purchase some fuzzy boots and warm sweaters to shove in my backpack.

Chapter 13

Ireland

My flight takes off to London and I've now been awake for about twenty-three hours. I'm sitting next to an Arabic couple with a young baby, but the baby is very sweet and quiet. I'm having a difficult time sleeping because the British stewardess is loud and keeps finding some way to wake me up. *I've seen the emergency flight plan hundreds of times! Don't single me out as someone who needs to wake up and listen to you! Two times now you've woken me up, and I'm exhausted.*

I arrive at Heathrow in London. The airport is large but easy to find my way through. I get to my Aer Lingus flight terminal and start conversations with some local Irish folk who are very friendly. I love their accents.

Two to three hours later, I arrive in Dublin with only seventy US dollars and a few dirhams in my pocket. At least I was wise enough to contact my credit card company to make them aware of my travels. I was unsure how much the seventy dollars would be worth after I exchanged it. It ends up being only worth forty-four euros. That'll buy me two T-shirts maybe.

I purchase a bus pass and jump on a double-decker. We ride by O'Connell Street up to the next bus station. I don't know where I'm supposed to find my hostel, but I know I will come close enough to walk. At least that's what I'm choosing to believe.

I exit the bus at a random location and take off by foot, asking people along the way until I find Jacob's Inn Hostel. I was right! I wasn't too far from my destination. Lucky guess!

I check into my hostel, where I'm sharing a room with nine other females.

It's funny how smooth it was finding my way here, but the little things like the different doorknobs, lighting fixtures, and currency are now becoming an interesting challenge. I didn't even know it was possible to open a door or turn on a light differently. It's all so standard in the United States.

I have two backpacks with me and need to get reorganized. I pull my clothes out and lay them on my bed. I don't have many things to wear, but there are still tags on some of the light sweaters I purchased in Dubai. I reorganize my plane tickets, itineraries, passport, and Iraqi entrance paperwork. I don't want to lose any of these documents along the way.

While unpacking, I see another young woman who is unpacking. Her name is Shawn, and she's traveling solo from Australia. We introduce ourselves and awkwardly ask if we should hang out since we're both alone. We decide it's a good idea, but we agree that we can go our separate ways if we choose.

Shawn is tall and thin with wavy brown hair. She has big brown eyes and a friendly, beautiful smile. While walking around the main streets, we talk about our stories a little bit and laugh about our differences in word usage. We frequently need to stop our conversation to explain ourselves. "What does that mean?" we ask each other.

We end up laughing at a couple of the terms that we don't understand yet are common in our respective homelands. My naivety causes me to overlook the possibility that common phrases would be different somewhere else. When I suggest something to do, she says, "I'm keen on that."

Shawn is an intriguing young woman in her midtwenties who is just out traveling the world on her own. She's spent her life in Australia and has a whole line up of countries to explore on her agenda. Before Ireland, she visited Scotland and Morocco, and she plans on living and working in Canada at a ski resort after her trip in Ireland. She's humble about her many recent travels, just soaking up all the culture and worldly knowledge that she can at this juncture in her life.

Her accent is really fun as well. It's one of those eloquent accents that presents as if she were very distinguished and intelligent. And yes, this is just another American perspective speaking.

We stroll down the busy street to the main strip and walk down a road that's packed with people shopping. The road is wide enough for cars to drive, but it's only accessible to foot traffic. Storefronts sit side by side along the whole strip and patrons continuously enter and exit with full shopping bags.

The weather is beautiful and fresh with puffy, white clouds. Shawn and I enter the Irish souvenir store, and I love everything green lined along the shelves. Knowing I have little room in my travel bags, I opt out of my urge to splurge.

We exit the souvenir store shortly after that and are surprised by a quick weather change to heavy rain. Umbrellas are open everywhere. I'm dressed appropriately for the location. I have a hood on my jacket, a scarf around my neck, like the rest of the crowd, and the fuzzy boots over my jeans.

Shawn and I keep laughing at ourselves for our common speculations of our surroundings. We see an old man stumble out of a pub and say, "Ahh … he looks like an authentic Irishman." He could be from Canada for all we know, but we're pretty set on our stereotypes.

We're now going to find what we deem as an authentic Irish pub so we can sit down and grab something for dinner. We see one on the corner and decide that's the one.

Everything in this pub is made of heavy wood: the floor, the bar, the chairs, and the tables. There is a fireplace and walls made of brick. I order a Guinness-steak pie with mashed potatoes and a Harp beer. It's the perfect food for a rainy and gray day in Ireland.

I'm very exhausted from travel and the time change. I'm used to Iraq time, which is two hours ahead of Ireland. I head back to the hostel and get ready for bed early. I lie down in bed #9 and pull the sheets up to my neck. The instant comfort makes me smile as I fall fast asleep.

It's a new day. Shawn and I will venture out on a guided walking tour of Dublin. After some breakfast of coffee and toast, our tour guide picks us up at the main entrance of the hostel. We set out to greet the chilly, clear-sky day. There are several more people to pick up along the way, so we stop at another hostel and proceed to walk another two miles to begin our tour at the Dublin Castle.

Our tour guide is a charismatic young man who is petite with blond hair and moves his arms around expressively as he speaks about the history of his beloved homeland. I'm captivated right away when he begins to speak of the history dating back to the early centuries AD and the influences of St. Patrick.

St. Patrick was a slave in Ireland for six years, beginning at age sixteen, when he was captured from Britain and taken from his family. After he escaped Ireland, he entered the church and became an ordained bishop. He later returned to Ireland with a message to spread.

St. Patrick camped up a high hill and lit a large bonfire. The fire summoned the king's interest, so he marched out to St. Patrick and asked what he was doing. It was at this time that St. Patrick used the three-leaf clover to introduce the king to Christianity. The three leaves, though separate in themselves, create one whole clover. Comparing the monotheism of Christianity, St. Patrick used the three leaves to describe the Holy Trinity: the Father, the Son, and the Holy Ghost. This was the beginning of the destiny that would solidify St. Patrick's name into history. He successfully brought Christianity to Ireland and spread the word of our Lord and Savior, Jesus Christ. The three-leaf clover became a great iconic image to their heritage. The date March 17 commemorates his death.

St Patrick's Day was traditionally observed without alcohol being drunk or sold because it was considered a holy day. Due to transformation by Western culture, it's now known for the copious consumption of alcohol accompanied by green beer and Jell-O shots.

During the rest of our walking tour, Shawn and I were introduced to the famous Temple Bar downtown and we were intrigued. After the tour, we stopped for lunch and did some shopping.

It's evening now. Shawn and I decide to get dressed up in our finest backpack-wrinkled attire and venture out for some beverages.

The pedestrian street is busy with tourists and locals alike. It's dark and the moon illuminates over the cobblestone alleys. Little pubs are all in a row on each side. As we walk past the different venues in the dark, we can peer into the lit-up pubs through the four-section windowpanes. I see a picturesque scene of jolly strangers coming together and raising glass mugs to the ceiling in a spontaneous celebratory moment. It looks so warm and happy inside each window I pass. We may hit up some of these locations later, but we came specifically to visit the Temple Bar.

We arrive to the Temple bar and squeeze into the door with all the rest of the folk. This place is packed and there's no opportunity for seating, barely room to even stand. We order what will be our only drink for the evening, because it takes forever to order more. I order a Guinness and she orders a Harp. We find a ledge to rest our beers on and enough room for our bodies to stand amid the packed crowd.

Back in the States, I've tried Guinness and I have to say that I don't care much for it, but I want to give it another try. I hold the pint of dark brew up to my lips and tip it toward my mouth for a taste. Wow! It tastes amazing. I'm surprised that I actually enjoy this beverage. Shawn and I observe the crowd while we sip on our drinks. Frothy, white rings remain inside my glass in a horizontal presentation with each encounter of the dark brew to my satisfied taste buds.

I love Dublin. It reminds me of home in many ways because of the temperate climate, but you can't ignore the dramatically different and deeper cultural roots attached to this city. While just walking along the busy streets, cultures collide. Literally! Someone who typically drives on the right side of the road (me) thinks they should also walk on the right side of the oncoming foot traffic, while individuals from London or Ireland are accustomed to driving and walking on the left side. The continuity of my pace and direction, while walking, is constantly being disrupted by this phenomenon as I am cut off and rerouted. I respond by being a good defensive walker and remaining calm.

It's a new day, and Shawn has left for a seven-day tour of Ireland. I'm on my own, and join the crowded street where hundreds of people are walking between stores. I set my pace relative to those next to me; otherwise, I would be mowing down pedestrians with my typical fast pace. I'm in the middle of this human-condensed location when a tall, dark man swoops up close to my side with a briefcase in hand. The sudden intrusion into my personal bubble makes me feel a little awkward so I pick up my pace. The man picks up his pace and stays close to my side.

"What is your name?" the man asks in a Swahili accent.

I pretend to ignore him and step between two oncoming people, trying to break free from what my discernment spoke as inappropriate. The man came near to me without missing a beat. "Where are you from?" he asks in a slightly demanding tone.

I'm in a crowd of hundreds of people yet somehow I suddenly feel secluded and unsafe at this moment. My mind races in fear as I again pick up my walking pace and try to ignore the strange, unsolicited questions. "What is your name?" he asks again, as if a nonresponse would never suffice.

"I'm Heidi," I lie, as if answering may free me of his presence.

Again, he asks, "Where are you from?"

"I'm from Canada and I have to go," I reply as I turn into a gift store. The man does not follow me.

Why the questions? Why was he following me as if no one else was around? I remember back to my trainings on human trafficking and all the different scenarios I learned about normal women being lured to side streets for abduction. This encounter did not feel like a normal curious stranger. This was a strange intrusion. Is it obvious that I'm alone?

When planning my Ireland trip, I had a difficult time deciding where to visit outside Dublin. I'm enjoying the city of Dublin, but I'm a huge fan of the outdoors and wanna take a drive somewhere else to see the countryside and check out another area. I have essentially one whole day and night that I allotted for a trip somewhere else.

I'm starting to regret not having a better plan as to where to visit because I feel like I'm wasting time "treading my tires" when I could be out seeing the sites.

In Ireland, they drive on the opposite side of the road from the United States and a lot of their rental cars are manual, meaning you steer from the right side of the car, on the left side of the road, and you shift with your left hand instead of your right. So much of driving is automatically programmed into our brain to where we hardly have to think about what we're doing. In fact, thinking may actually inhibit the natural instincts of such an automatic skill. I thought that renting a car might be a fun challenge while experiencing the countryside.

After a little reading up on the car rentals, I chicken out due to lack of time and being unsure if I will qualify for rental insurance with my credit card. Too many unknowns and too little time to run around making decisions, so I will just put on my backpack and walk across the street from my hostel to the bus station.

Hmm, where to go? I saw pictures of Galway in my little Ireland travel book and thought it looked like a quaint little town that I would like to visit.

I buy a ticket from the machine and am happy to see that the next bus to Galway is leaving in less than thirty minutes. Perfect! I stand in line with the rest of the crowd and wait.

Today is the day of the Ireland marathon, an event I so badly wanted to take part in. I actually registered for the event, hoping I could train for it while I was in Iraq. I found it difficult to go on long runs outside of my firehouse in Taji because of the need to stay close to the fire engine in case we got a call.

My cardiovascular strength is awesome and I figured I would just prepare my body and mind for the long 26.2-mile "race" by treadmill only. I hoped that I could start out my first event with a 10 K or a half marathon, but the Ireland marathon just offered that: a marathon. After training for a while, I felt great doing six miles. I felt great, that is until, I got off the treadmill and my feet were hurting. I recognized this feeling. This happened to me last summer when I announced I was going to train for the Honolulu marathon. I got up to six miles and the fascia of my feet started to get real sore and difficult to stand on. I'm already battling a tightened hip flexor muscle from neglecting my stretching and then I could barely even walk on my darn feet. The marathon was off the list yet again. Well, maybe someday I'll accomplish this goal somewhere else.

The bus driver arrives late due to the large crowds of marathoners preparing for their run, but it isn't long before we're on the road.

What a beautiful day. The rain wore off, and the sunshine is peeking out.

I get myself comfy in the large bus seat and sit back to enjoy the views. It would be so fun to drive a rental car right now, but this is a much more relaxing scenario.

Just as we leave the city, I witness the rolling green hills of the countryside and the abundance of farm animals. The grass is a beautiful green. *It seems a little different from the green on the west coast of the United States,* I think, *almost a brighter green like you would find in your childhood Easter basket.*

The pastures are nourished with vegetation and I can see rocks peeking out from under the soil. I laugh to myself, thinking about how difficult it probably is to dig into that soil. My house in Washington has horribly rocky soil and I can relate to the frustration of gardening in rocky terrain.

The fields are full of sheep and horses and cows and more sheep, all fenced in by hand-built rock fences. I imagine this type of fence was a resourceful way of utilizing many of the large stones from under their property. Occasionally, I spot an old castle or large building made of all stone, some of which appear to be partially crumbled down, giving off a historical, renaissance feel.

The trip takes about three hours, and the good weather trend continues throughout the ride. We make several stops along the way in quaint little villages. I'm tempted to get off at some of these bus stops because it's so beautiful here.

During the last hour of the ride, the bus veers from the main highway and is en route via the winding, narrow back roads. There are sheep everywhere, and at times, I'm surprised to see the bus squeeze past other cars and trucks on these tiny, old side streets.

We gradually leave the countryside to enter a small city. Just as gradually, the sun seems to fade away and the wet streets reflect their recent encounter with precipitation. I notice an eerie emptiness in these little towns, and the trend continues as we arrive in Galway. I overhear another passenger talking about an Irish Bank holiday.

A bank holiday? Well, what luck, I think sarcastically. Even though it's a weekday, I can see that many stores are closed and few people are around.

We roll into a dreary, empty Galway, and I think, *Of all the stops we've made along the way, this is the one I'm departing to? Ugh!*

"Well, I'm going to enjoy this place as best as I can," I self-encourage as I don my backpack with determination.

Okay, first step is to find a hostel to check into. As I step off the bus, I spot a big sign that shows me the way to a nearby hostel. I had an awesome experience at the hostel in Dublin despite the concerns from many friends asking me, "Haven't you seen the movie?" as they were referring to the horror movie called *Hostel*. "No," I would reply, "that's why I don't watch scary movies. I don't want them to ruin my good time."

I enter the old building and walk up to the front desk. The staff and surroundings emanate an alternative feel, yet friendly and welcoming.

"One bed for the night, please," I pipe to the long-haired man behind the desk. I pay in euros and he gives me a room number and a pass code for entrance.

I creak up the narrow wooden staircase and enter the ten-person room. It seems nice enough, except I look over and notice two guys in the room. Well, yes, I live with a bunch of boys at my firehouse in Iraq, but this is a little different. I'm not comfortable or accustomed to such arrangements and realize now that I didn't ask for a female-only dormitory. Oops! Well, maybe it'll be okay. I put my backpack in the locker under the bed and take only my purse so that I can walk around town for a while.

It's midday and the sky is a dark gray. There's a chill in the air. I walk up a couple of blocks and find a rather unusual mall entrance. It looks as if I'm walking down into a parking garage.

I enter the mall and realize how hungry I am, so I order a sandwich and soup from a little café inside. My food is then brought over to me and I sit alone, eating, noticing that I'm getting a lot of looks from the locals. I wonder if I stand out as a solo traveler, or are they looking at me because I'm eating alone? Why do I feel like people are looking at me?

I begin to think about how uncommon it is for women in the United States to go and eat meals alone at restaurants. I wonder if it's the same here in this culture. Of course, there are situations where one would eat alone, but we usually take it to go if we are forced to eat alone. No bother. I want to relax and eat my food. I really don't feel uncomfortable being alone, but when you think of something as much as I am right now, you begin to look guilty of feeling the particular way that you are thinking—if that makes sense. Maybe I'm giving off the perception of discomfort because I'm not eating confidently by myself. Hmm …

After eating solo, I partake in a little bit of clothes shopping. I find a few stylish items to shove in my backpack that will wear nice for my trip to Switzerland and Italy. I'm really enjoying this whole shopping in foreign countries thing. Besides having been in the desert, where uniformity in attire is commonplace, I really enjoy seeing the styles in these other countries and knowing that I'm adding them to my American wardrobe. Shopping isn't necessarily what I envisioned for my European travels, considering I could shop anywhere and I have a tendency to be a bit of a tightwad with my finances. I realize this, but it's a gray day and I decide to give myself a break and just enjoy the time for a few hours.

After wearing myself out from shopping, I head back to the hostel. I sit on the bed in my shared room and contemplate my evening. Hmm … go out for drinks? Nah, not by myself, not tonight.

Hmm ... I don't know what else there is to do on a bank holiday in this town. I begin to think about my comfy hostel bed back in Dublin. In fact, hostels are so inexpensive that I still have my bed reserved there and could conceivably head back and stay there. Not that this place isn't nice; I'm just not really feeling it for this particular day.

My mind is made up. I'm going to walk to the bus station and use my return ticket just three hours after my arrival.

The nice man at the desk with the long hair gives me my sixteen euros back since I didn't use the bed and I'm headed back to the bus stop.

Now here I am back at the bus stop, and the wait for the bus is long this evening. The line starts out short and gradually gets longer and longer. A bunch of young people are heading to Dublin. I didn't realize that this was a college town. A lot of the students are probably out of town because of the holiday. The majority of people in line for the bus are college age, early twenties/late teens.

The sun is setting and it's getting chilly. Two buses pull up to the curb, and there's suddenly a discrepancy as to where the front of the line is and who's going on what bus. The people who stood in line for over an hour want to have their rightful spot as first to board the bus, while the people who haven't been in line as long all of a sudden notice the opportunity to push their way into a more advantageous position.

I find my way onto the bus and decide it would be fun to sit in the very front seat, opposite the driver's side. The driver's seat is on the right side of the bus, and I have a full view out the front window from the left side of the bus. The men that drove the buses up to the curb are no longer on duty, so we have to wait for our real bus drivers to get here.

Yet another wait is upon us as we anticipate the arrival of our chauffer for the evening. It's dark outside and a red-haired man jumps into the seat wearing the traditional Irish flat cap upon his head.

"Where's my feckin wing man?" the driver asks himself irritably in his thick brogue. He starts the engine and begins the drive to Dublin.

I'm excited to sit in the front seat and view the road from the opposite side through the large bus window. I lean forward in anticipation. As we take off, the irritation of the man driving becomes palpable and reflects in the maneuvering of each turn in the road. He's on his cell phone and driving with one hand on the wheel. Corners are being cut tightly and taken quickly.

The apparatus is completely filled with passengers in every seat. The body heat of the crowd and adversary-outdoor cold conceives a product of steam on the windows, obstructing the view of the windshield. My anticipation of a fun bus ride takes me from edge of the seat in excitement to slumping back and looking at the windshield in disdain, as if it's going to meet me up front and personal at any moment.

Now the man has one hand on the wheel, cell phone between ear and shoulder, and one hand frantically searching for the defrost feature. It begins to rain outside. It's pitch dark and we are swerving over the lines on the side of the road. As our driver is searching for the defrost button, he flips a switch that turns on the headlights. So we've been riding in the dark with our headlights off? I gaze, open mouthed, as I notice a caution sign for sheep crossing and think, *I may never see my family again. I'm going to die right here on this bus.*

The driver finally gets the windows cleared up and I decide it's time for me to shut my eyes and just sleep the rest of the ride.

After 2200 (10:00 p.m.), we're dropped off in downtown Dublin, not the bus station across from my hostel. This particular area of town is a main street that's well lit and full of people. I learned the day prior that this is the street that divides the so-called good side of town and the bad side of town.

I'm quite a ways from my hostel right now and feeling thankful that I've become familiar with Dublin over the previous couple of days. I would be in big trouble navigating with my lack of direction sense during this time of the night if I hadn't become familiar.

Departing the well-lit street, I turn down another main street that is typically filled with people and is now desolate. My backpack and I have about a mile to go and I'm walking as quickly as I can down the vacant storefront corridor. I glance briefly into each alleyway as I pass by and hope to steer clear of any trouble.

As I negotiate my way down the darkened streets and pass narrow alleyways, I see the light of my hostel in view, beckoning me back to comfort.

My body and mind are filled with joy and relief as I crawl into bed #9 in my room tonight. It feels great to close my eyes and enjoy a well-earned slumber.

Chapter 14

Switzerland

I BOARD A PLANE FROM THE green countryside of Ireland, Alex flies from the dry deserts of the United Arab Emirates, and we meet in the middle at snowy Zurich, Switzerland. We're going to be staying in Zermatt, so we need to hop some trains.

Switzerland is adjacent to France, Italy, and close to Germany. Because of the location, I know the language barriers I might encounter will be German, French, and Italian. Neither Alex nor I speak these languages, so train hopping from Zurich to Zermatt is a cultural experience in itself. Random people start small conversations with us in German, Italian, or French, and we stand wide-eyed and confused.

Being that we've never utilized the train system before, we want to make sure we transfer trains in the right towns. We pass by people, asking if any of them speak English. After a while, we manage to hop the right trains.

We've taken three different trains now, and we're not quite sure if we backtracked a little bit along the way.

Finally, we wait at the transfer station for our last train ride. All of the trains have looked alike so far, until we see an old rickety red train pull up.

No way. Is this our train? We wonder. This train car must be a hundred years older than all the others we've seen, and it's much smaller.

We're the only people to board the train. It's empty. The quaint old upholstery of the seats is very outdated and reminds me of something I would have deemed "old" back when I was a kid. We sit down by the window seats and the train screeches as it starts up the track.

I've enjoyed the views of Switzerland by train, but this leg of the trip is absolutely breathtaking. Large, snowy mountains frame the backdrop of peaceful valleys. Four-story chalets are wrapped with carved-wooden balconies at each level of the home. Farm animals and orchards are abundant and appear to accompany the landscape of every home. Some homes are shingled with large pieces of slate. I'm fascinated by the architecture.

We pass by green valleys and the train begins to ascend into the snowy mountains. Our train screams up the tracks while it zigzags past rivers and streams. It reminds me of the train that said, "I think I can, I think I can." We laugh at the slower pace and loud scream from our old, red train trying to make its way up the mountain. It's exciting to ride in this transportation apparatus, even though it seems to have degraded structural integrity.

Finally, we make it to Zermatt, which is only accessible by train. You get around in this village by foot or horse carriage. We walk off the train and it seems as if no one is around; the town appears uninhabited. We head down a stone pathway until we see the sign for what we hope is our hotel. It's a little later in the evening and we meander up the narrow, twisted staircase to the lobby. The lobby is dark and the door is locked with a closed sign on the front.

"I think this is our hotel," I say to Alex. I forgot to print off the name of the hotel or the directions to get to it, so I'm pretty pleased that we only had to walk a short distance from the train station to find what I believe is our hotel.

Alex appears concerned. Right next to the door is a wooden board that has hooks with room numbers next to them. One of the hooks has a key dangling from it.

"Look." I point at the key. "That's probably our room key."

We take the key and open the door to the room it correlates with. Although I'm fairly certain the key has been left for us, Alex is impressed with how pragmatic yet spontaneous I am about the whole situation.

"I like to have plans, but I don't like to stress if things don't necessarily go as I expect," I say to him.

The view from our little room is breathtaking. It seems as if you could reach your arm out over the snow-covered roof and grab the peak of the Matterhorn, break it off, and take a bite of it. We're so close to the rugged, majestic mountain peak.

Zermatt is a cute little snowy village in the mountains and there are several restaurants and stores within a hundred yards of our hotel. It's time to find a restaurant to eat at, after our long day of travel.

Even though it isn't our first time ever going to a restaurant, there's a slight uncertainty when walking in because we don't know if there are differences culturally in any of the seating arrangements or dress code. We're dressed as travelers who arrived in a backpack from the desert and just picked up a couple of random winter clothes along the way. The restaurant is a little bit fancy for our attire, but we're warmly greeted and seated at a table in the nearly empty dining area.

The first thought that came to me is *Yes! I finally get to have my first glass of red wine in months.* Of course, I could've had wine in Ireland, but I was too busy enjoying the Guinness and wanted to drink what I deemed culturally relevant to my location. Alex mentions that he tried a glass of wine before and doesn't care for it. He thinks he'll order a beer instead.

I order a glass of cabernet sauvignon from the waiter and he returns with a bottle. The man presents the bottle of wine to me by holding one hand lightly at the bottom and one hand at the neck of the bottle to show me the label. Respectfully and delicately, he pours a small amount of the juicy, red wine into my glass. Now, I love my wine, but I am not a wine connoisseur and my exposure to the techniques of appropriate wine tasting is limited. My style of consumption typically is a little bit primitive in comparison to those that take a moment to appreciate the fine art of wine. I quickly remember to my first wine-tasting experience with my best friend. When we were twenty-one years old, we received a little bit of advice on wine tasting etiquette 101. I gently swirl the wine in my glass and put it up to my nose. I sniff the aromas from the glass as if I might be able to decipher any of the berries or tannins from the subtle aroma. I take a small mouthful of the wine, allowing it to roll over my tongue.

"It's really good," I state my approval. The waiter fills up my glass and proceeds to fill Alex's glass. We both tense up for a moment as if to decide whether or not it would be rude to tell him not to pour another glass. We say nothing as the waiter fills our glasses, sets the bottle on our table, and then walks off.

"Well, I guess you're drinking wine tonight." I state the obvious. Alex takes a sip and is pleasantly surprised that it's a good-tasting glass of wine. This is where we learn that you cannot just order a glass of wine. When you order wine in this part of the world, the only option is to buy the whole bottle. I'm happy with that idea. There will be no wishy-washy decisions of whether or not to order a second glass and maybe feel guilty about it. It's definitive that I will be having at least one more glass.

We continue to enjoy our bottle of wine as we're served bread with mozzarella and tomatoes, drizzled in olive oil and balsamic vinegar. Bread, wine, and cheese are my weakness, and this is so delicious. Next, the pizza is served with pepperoni and olives. I glance at the pizza and notice that instead of sliced olives scattered atop the cheese, there are full olives. The olives are complete with the pit inside and all. I peel the olive skin off the pit and scatter it on my slice of pizza. I take a bite of the pizza and taste the fresh saltiness of the olive. I'm amazed at how much more superb a full olive tastes in comparison to the sliced, pitted, canned olives that I'm accustomed to. This difference alone makes the pizza amazing. It's a thin crust and the basil, meat, and cheese are so fresh. The whole meal is amazing, and it's a great way to finish a day of plains and trains.

After dinner, Alex and I walk hand in hand down the stone path, back to our cozy little suite. Months after our first conversation in Texas and daily correspondents on the computer, Alex and I justify our time spent as an approval for us to waste no time in becoming intimate. I'm content to finally be in his presence and in his arms.

Morning arrives and I'm awakened by the beautiful ringing of church bells from nearby. I fall back to sleep.

Several minutes later, the bells ring again. This time they ring continuously for several minutes. *Well, that's kind of a nice way to wake up*, I think. It's like an alarm clock and a snooze button. I lie in bed enjoying the peaceful bells and begin to notice they aren't stopping.

After they ring for a while, the steady dinging and donging becomes louder and faster and almost off key, if that's possible to say for the tone of a bell. The bells are beginning to ring obnoxiously as if to say, "Get out of bed right now!" There's really no sleeping in after that.

We spend the whole day walking around Zermatt, viewing the Matterhorn, and visiting little touristy stores. Of course, you can't go to Switzerland and not eat chocolate. We find a picturesque candy store and point at all the chocolates as the lady behind the counter runs back and forth filling up our bag with all the milk-chocolaty goodness that catches our eye. It's kind of an expensive bag of chocolates by the time we're done, but so worth it. We pay for our indulgence in Swiss francs and thank the women behind the counter. They speak English well and are fairly easy to communicate with. They say their courtesies in German. *Danke!* (Thank you!)

Zermatt is an expensive place because of the isolated location. Simple sweatshirts are priced around three hundred Swiss francs, and the American dollar is fairly close in comparison to the franc. We find a McDonald's disguised as a log cabin and that's where we end up having several of our meals.

All businesses in this town shut down at noon for one hour, so if shopping is to be done, you're out of luck during that lunch hour. I take the opportunity to purchase a souvenir Swiss bell while the shops are open.

Back in Iraq, one of the jobs that Alex and I had to do was destroy and refill various kinds of fire extinguishers. Because of the hundreds of extinguishers we have evaluated over time, we are both in the habit of inspecting. There's a blue fire extinguisher in the stairwell of our Zermatt hotel that both Alex and I silently turn our heads toward every time we pass, going up and down the stairs. Without even speaking of it, I know that he and I are continuously and habitually conducting fire inspections of all our locations.

After a few days in Switzerland, I'm sad to leave, but anxious to get to Italy. I soak up the rest of the Swiss landscape from the window seat of the train as we head toward a different country. When we cross the Italian border, the train stops and our passports are checked by the Italian *polizia*. A short ride later, we arrive in Milan, Italy. Milano, Italia!

Chapter 15

Italy

Burnt orange and yellow-green hues blush the backdrop of the tree line and one cannot deny that it is autumn here in Europe. It's crispy, fresh, and exhilarating to be outdoors in Italy.

We weren't initially planning a trip to Milan. This is a random last-minute decision because the ticket salesman in Zermatt swore that no trains would be running within Italy due to a strike and that we would have to arrive and stay in a border town. His concern about a railway strike had us wondering if we would even be making it to our departure city of Rome to return to the desert. Well, all trains are running just fine in Italy, without any strikes, so we are taken on a tangent just for giggles I suppose.

The first thing that needs to be done in Milan is to purchase our train tickets for tomorrow to Firenze (Florence). Alex holds our bags as I wait in line at the ticket kiosk. The bustling crowd of European travelers is beginning to impose a feeling of overstimulation upon me as I look frantically at travel options to Florence on the computer-screen ticket kiosk.

"They're all booked up," I lip to Alex silently across the rows of people in line.

"What?" he lips back to me.

I turn back toward the kiosk and I'm feeling pressured and stressed from the impatient patrons behind me. I've already taken up enough of their precious time trying to figure out which national flag to push for my language preference. Of course, I was looking for the American flag option (which is not available), overlooking the British flag which would have led me through the kiosk options in English as well.

Well, I suppose we'll have to select the lower-class tickets and stand in the baggage area. Purchasing tickets to Florence via train should not be done on short notice, apparently.

We at least have reservations for a hotel which we booked online. The language barrier is still our biggest obstacle to quickly finding our whereabouts, but an exciting challenge to the adventure.

Milan is full of stone statues and flowing fountains intertwined with multistory residential and business buildings that house the large population of this bustling metropolis. After finding ourselves unable to communicate with several people, we find someone that is able to explain how we get to our hotel. *"Grazie,"* I reply as we walk away with the explanation clinging precariously in our short-term memories.

After checking into our hotel, we set out again to what would be pretty much the daily highlight of our trip: dinnertime.

We arrive to a dimly lit restaurant with a lobster tank toward the entrance. The gentleman smiles at our attempts to exchange dialect. The Italian man has a calm and patient demeanor; he seems to be very used to the inability to share common language with his customers.

We order pizza and pasta along with a bottle of Chianti. While ordering, Alex questions the man about the pasta entrée. Somewhere in the middle of the repeated questioning with rewording to create understanding, Alex quits speaking English and begins speaking Spanish. Before I know what's going on, the two of them are holding a conversation, smiling and laughing with understanding.

"What just happened?" I ask. Apparently, Italian and Spanish are similar enough that they're able to understand one another. Our language barrier issue should no longer be an issue for the rest of our tour of Italy.

After our amazing Italian meal, the man brings around a fancy dessert tray and names off the items. Midway through the selections, he points at a big log-shaped dessert and calls it cheesecake.

"What?" Alex and I interject simultaneously.

He repeats himself with assurance and a smile. Alex and I are quick to order a piece of the strange-looking cheesecake. The thick, creamy contents are rolled like a cinnamon roll with the thin, delicate crust swirled through it. It's topped off with a drizzle of raspberry sauce. This is by far the best cheesecake I've ever encountered.

The next day, Alex and I randomly walk the streets of Milan, looking at architecture and meandering through flea markets. Among other fresh caught fish, giant swordfish heads lie on beds of ice with long, sword-like noses piercing the air. Flowers, fruit, and Italian leather are the common theme on the streets. Inside the butcher shops, there are giant ham hocks hanging from the ceiling while corner wine shops sell various cheeses and fancy-shaped wine bottles. We walk casually down the cobblestone streets in contentment with our inspiring surroundings.

After Milan, we travel by train to Florence and experience the feeling of being second-class citizens while squeezing in the baggage area. We find ourselves near the narrow stairs of the exit door. The stairs are too narrow to comfortably sit down, and then you can't see out the window. Who wants to travel through Italy and not look out the window? So we make do with standing for a couple of hours, while hanging on to the metal pole nearby.

It's a dreary and gray day in Florence, but we don't waste any time in sightseeing. Our bags are dropped off at the hotel room and we set out with nothing but ourselves and our wallets. We choose a direction and begin to walk. The air is cool and it begins to rain. Luckily for us, there are people selling umbrellas on every street corner. It's obvious there's a large market here for umbrella sales to all the unprepared tourists.

We don't know where we're going, but we follow the crowded streets of people hoping to make a discovery. The rain stops and the sky clears up. As we round a corner, we enter a crowded piazza and look up in amazement to see the breathtaking cathedral: Basilica di Santa Maria del Fiore. The church stands up high against the skyline as the facade of marble and sandstone shows meticulously from the ground up. Tiny marble statues stand in the exterior wall along with many shapes and intricate details. The tiny statues stand in such a way that it appears as if there are people standing on windowsills, peering down at you.

Alex and I join a tour group to visit the local art museums. We also take a bus tour of the Tuscany countryside. The olive trees up in the hills must look beautiful when the sun is shining, only I'm viewing them through large water dollops clinging to the glass on my bus window. I have to envision what their beauty holds through this kaleidoscopic view.

Alex and I are having a great cultural experience together. We're getting along well and seeing some amazing sites, but it feels as though we aren't necessarily in sync with one another as much as we had anticipated. Over the last few months, we've had a passionate Internet dating relationship and now we find ourselves in some awkwardness as we try to actually get to know one another in person. I'm not able to completely relax and show him who I am, and he's not really opening up to me either.

We board our final train of the vacation and leave Florence to head toward Rome. Roma, Italia!

As we jump on the train and stand in the baggage area with the rest of the second classers, I look out the door and see an Italian couple embracing one another. The couple displays their farewells to one another by kissing passionately. It's one of those moments you wish you could see more often. Not the young, obnoxious, preteen kissing but adults kissing like they love one another. The type of kiss you see in a movie when true love and passion exist. I long for that moment, that loving embrace. Maybe Alex and I will reach that stage in our relationship, or maybe we won't meet the hype of our previous expectations at all.

We reach our swanky hotel by taxi from the train station. It isn't close to the station or the airport, which we tried to do at our previous stays. Since we're moving about our European destinations in a somewhat unplanned and sporadic fashion, we hoped to stay near prime transportation so we wouldn't have any issues getting around with ease. For our stay in Rome, we find it difficult to find a hotel we can book the night prior online, so we chose one that is decently priced but uniquely designed.

As every hotel on our trip, there are two twin beds pushed together to create one large bed. The walls in the rooms are a chic frosted glass that makes the room look modern and fresh. There are various colored and shaped light fixtures arranged in an abstract and decorative fashion. Although it's a good price to stay here, it feels as if we're residing in an expensive and luxurious suite.

After our hotel check-in, it's necessary to head back out into the city to acquire some dinner. The sun has long gone down and there are many people out and about once we reach what we think must be the center of the city. We bring along our umbrellas that we purchased on the street corners of Florence. The rain comes and goes and the streets glisten. When the rain falls, the streets appear blanketed with a protective shell of multicolored umbrellas, covering the tourists who are out and determined to venture in spite of precipitation.

We're amazed when we see large ancient buildings gated in with fountains and marble statues. Our pursuit of Rome is with an adventurous spirit and a lack of education on the history and presence of art. It's a little unfortunate that we're unable to identify some of these amazing structures or the history behind them.

We've been walking for miles with no exact destination in mind. I look up ahead in the dark and see a golden light gently illuminating a structure in the distance. I clear my eyes and peer toward the structure more intently. My heart races with excitement.

"Is that the Colosseum?" I ask Alex as I point ahead.

"I think it is!" he replies with a definite increase in excitement to his own voice.

We acquire a little more of a hop in our step as we head through the darkness toward the golden light. "I can't believe that's really it!" I continue in my giddiness. I knew that we would see the Colosseum during our time here, but something about this moment, this unexpected siting, makes me feel beyond amazed. This is a moment I will surely never forget.

Today we will be taking a tour of Rome and the Colosseum with a group. You can get into places quicker when you sign up for a tour. Alex and I saw a daunting line of people wrapping around a building earlier and we feel smart for not taking that route.

Last night, we got up next to the Colosseum and saw it lit up in the dark. I can't wait to see the inside of it during the day and hear about all the history.

Earth-tone shades of gray, white, and brown mix beautifully in the ancient architecture that is set high upon a peaceful baby-blue sky. Intricately detailed columns of stone and marble show the care and detail from the Roman hands. This craftsmanship took more time, blood, and sweat than anyone nowadays could imagine. Large pillars and structures stand tall, seemingly touching the skyline. Some pieces have fallen down while others stand tall, holding their ancient and majestic appeal.

Our tour guide walks us inside the Colosseum and tells us about the architecture of the warrior pit below. It used to contain two levels: one where the animal or warrior would wait below and then the actual fighting arena above. Man would fight beast, and man would fight man. The bloody sport would go on for hours and days with many deaths and defeats. Millions could sit on their marble seats to watch the event.

After invasions and destruction of the ages, only a few marble seats remain. The facility had many marble statues back in the early ages but they were looted and damaged. This Colosseum was a sight to see in its prime, and now it's a historical piece still standing tall and proud.

What a beautiful night in Rome. We sit down at a restaurant outside on the piazza. There's an acoustic of ancient sculpted fountains flowing water with a harmonious accompaniment by the sound of a traditional Italian mandolin. The dark sky is upon us with a romantic candle-lit ambiance and we're warmed by the radiant heat of a stainless-steel propane lamp. If I could be anywhere on my last night in Rome, this would be it.

The tremolo of a traditional Italian mandolin strums romantically in the backdrop. The delicate flavors of cheese, bread, and olives pair perfectly with our Chianti red wine. I feel like this moment could only be this perfect in the movies.

When our wine glasses empty, the maître d' arrives in perfect timing to pour the bottle for us, even though we could easily pour it ourselves. Conversations would only take away from this moment. Alex and I are beyond content sitting in silence and soaking up the environment.

"Alex, what time is it?" I shake his shoulder aggressively as he sleeps.

I just woke up and I know we're going to the airport this morning. I shouldn't be waking up before an alarm clock.

Alex pops up. "Oh crap! I didn't set the alarm clock."

We leap out of bed and commence Operation Chaos as we throw our unpacked items into bags.

"Umm, we need to call a taxi too." I mention.

If we'd packed our clothes the night before, we probably could've fit everything in our backpacks. Since we're desperately shoving balled-up clothing into backpacks, we have to quickly decide what to keep and what to leave behind. This feels like a fire drill because we almost don't have enough time to grab anything. We are so late!

The pessimist in me comes out. "I don't think we're gonna make it."

In sheer panic, we zip our backpacks and lunge out the door in a sprint toward the front desk. Alex speaks in Spanish to the Italian workers and asks them to quickly call us a taxi.

A few minutes waiting feels like hours as our taxi driver pulls up. We aren't even close to the airport. Time ticks by and I'm now worried I will lose my job if I miss my flight.

Wow, I didn't realize we were this far away. The taxi driver speeds down the highway, and we're still not there. I think our plane is boarding already.

We pull up to the airport.

"Umm ... I don't think this is the right entrance." I again hesitate to bring more negativity to the current situation.

The taxi driver circles us away and keeps driving to another entrance that looks a little more promising.

"Okay, we'll get out here."

We grab our backpacks and dash inside to the front desk where no one else is in line. We each have two backpacks now, so we can only carry one and have to check the other through. Mine needs to go to Dubai, and Alex's needs to arrive in Texas. The lady at the counter doesn't think our baggage will make it on the plane in time; in fact, she doesn't think we'll make our flight at all and she doesn't seem very sympathetic. She points us in the direction of our flight.

Alex and I sprint at our maximum pace, not having any sense of how long we will have to run. My heart squeezes and cramps up, but peer pressure takes precedence and I have to keep up with Alex. I don't like being the weak link, so I keep going. We are at an all-out sprint with our backpacks on, and I start to get dizzy right as we arrive at our gate.

People are standing calmly outside the gate as we arrive panting and drenched in sweat.

"Is this the flight to London?" I ask.

"Yes," replies the man.

Alex and I sit down on a bench and catch our breath. I'm so happy and surprised that we didn't miss our flight. My pleasure, however, is tempered by a red face and irritating back sweat. Not to mention it's rather anticlimactic to arrive in such an extreme panic to discover we totally have time left.

I'm impressed that throughout our suspenseful morning hotel evacuation, neither Alex nor I argued or lost our temper. We were both notably irritated of the situation but didn't once lose focus on the pursuit of arriving to our departure flight in one piece. Maybe that's the firefighter in us—staying focused on the mission.

Ahh, we have good seats in an exit row, which means plenty of legroom. This is great. The flight attendant has a seat next to ours during takeoff and she enquires about our destinations. We proceed to tell her about our little romantic adventure and how we now have to part ways. We don't even know how long it will be until we see each other again.

After takeoff, the stewardess stands up and proceeds to her work duties. She comes back to us with two little bottles of Champagne and plastic flutes in hand. She smiles as she hands us the beverages.

"This is complimentary from us to you. Thank you for helping the soldiers over there."

"Wow, thank you!" we say as we smile back at her.

I feel guilty taking any credit helping the soldiers, because I have ultimate faith that our troops are beyond capable to do the duties we do. I'm just thankful for the opportunity to work with them. I can only hope it somehow makes a difference.

Alex and I finally are able to relax and smile now. We pour each other a glass of Champagne and I pour some of our breakfast orange juice into the glass as well. We celebrate a toast to our adventures and drink up our mimosas.

Our plane arrives to London later than scheduled, and Alex is now concerned about making his connection flight on time. I still have plenty of time for my flight.

Once we touch foot in the London airport, we kiss good-bye and part ways quickly. I don't know when I will see Alex again. I hope he makes his flight on time.

Chapter 16

Back to the Desert

For my flight home, which is Iraq, I'm dressed comfortably in my black leggings and tan, curve-hugging sweater that I bought in Ireland. I'm also wearing the fuzzy boots from Dubai, which will be easy to slip off and on. I was thinking I would dress in comfortable lightweight clothing so that I can pass through security easily. No buckles or bulky pockets full of coins.

While passing through London airport security, I feel comfortable and quick when I slip off my boots and backpack to pass them through the scan machine. I'm in a long line and it's my turn to walk through the body scan device. I walk through and the alert sound goes off.

Well, that's weird, I think. I've caused a sudden stall in the line behind me as the woman attending has me pass through again. Again, the alert sound goes off. She seems confused as well because my cotton skin-hugging outfit leaves little for one to imagine what metal objects would be present. She pats me down aggressively while consulting with the female worker next to her.

The ATF has recently increased their level of security at these points and they're touching around all areas of my body without much modesty. She waves the sensor wand across my body and stops at my breast. She sets the wand to the side and proceeds to cup my breasts underneath with both hands. In context, I understand what she's searching for, but out of context, it's quite awkward as she unknowingly jiggles my breasts while turning her head to tell her counterpart that she thinks it's just my underwire. I have to giggle at the awkward situation because we're standing around many impatient people, and the woman doesn't let go of her cupped hands while she pauses to contemplate and then jiggles again. She concludes that I'm setting off the alert with my bra and lets me proceed to pick up my boots and carryon.

I arrive to Dubai late in the evening and I know there are a shuttle and a hotel room waiting for me. I'm looking for my other backpack and it's not coming around the conveyer belt. Everyone else from the flight finds their bags, and I still have no bag.

After filling out the missing-luggage paperwork, I miss my shuttle and am stuck waiting at the airport. Ugh! I could be asleep in my hotel room right now.

It's midnight and I walk outside to find myself the only female among dozens of Middle Eastern men, all wearing variations of robes and head pieces. I'm intimidated and scared by some of the looks I'm receiving. I wish I hadn't missed the shuttle.

I ask the man at the outdoor podium if the shuttle is coming back again soon. After learning they won't be able to pick me up until 0200 (2:00 a.m.), the Middle Eastern man offers to give me a ride in an hour when he's off work.

"No thank you. I should wait for my company to come get me." *What a sketchy proposition,* I think. *I can't see that ending well.*

I find a seat inside the airport and wait. I doze off in the chair and am awoken by a man who arrives to pick me up along with two other contractors. What a relief!

I'll be staying one more night in Dubai before I fly back to Baghdad. After I was picked up at the airport last night, I got to my hotel room and slept soundly. Today I'm going to walk across the street to the mall and see what I can do with my time.

After living in the desert for several months, my stringy, dirty-blonde hair has gotten out of control; I have to do something about it. I walk into a small salon in the mall and am greeted by the Filipina woman standing by the sink.

"Do you do blonde highlights?" I ask the woman.

She pulls her chin in toward her neck and scrunches her eyebrows down. "Your hair color? No!" she responds as if I've lost my mind.

"Okay, I'll just get a trim," I compromise.

Well, the trim ends up being a botch job. End of story.

It's not too big of a deal though. I have to laugh at myself for my chronic inability to obtain the fully glamorized look that I admire in other women. I'm so good at getting close to looking like a classy young twenty-eight-year-old but can't seem to hide the slight remnants of my tomboy side. I enjoy looking nice, but I also love feeling confident enough to head out casual, in just jeans and a T-shirt.

When I return to the hotel room, I hear someone call out my name. *Do I know anyone in Dubai right now?* I wonder.

I look down the hallway to see one of my lieutenants from Taji. I love running into people over here. It's the coolest part of the trip.

He and I walk down the sidewalk to a pub to catch up over some chicken wings and a beer. I remember my first trip to Dubai when I was afraid to have even a sip of beer. I'm not as concerned anymore, now that I'm more familiar with the location.

Tomorrow I fly back to Baghdad, and I'll probably have to wait there for a couple of days before I catch my mil-air flight to Taji.

I enjoyed my vacation but I'm happy to be back at my base. I still haven't gotten my other backpack yet. It must've gotten lost in Rome.

My Taji brother Mocoso left Iraq because it was the end of his one-year contract and he left me the map that was hanging on his wall. It's a map of the world and I'm eager to put pushpins into the different countries that I've traveled to. In less than six months, I've visited five new countries in Europe and the Middle East. I've officially caught the travel bug. I placed a pin in Iraq, United Arab Emirates, Ireland, Switzerland, and Italy. I can't officially count England, even though I passed through the London airport twice. It doesn't count for me unless I leave the building.

Now I want to go to Thailand, I think.

I found out about a travel company that facilitates you through journeys that can include animal riding, hiking, biking, home stays with locals, and other endeavors you may not be able to recreate on your own as a traveler. The vacation I want to plan includes an elephant ride into the jungle then you eat and stay with a local family for a night, ride a bicycle through monkey territory, visit the Bangkok flea market, and sample fried bugs. All the reservations would be completely hassle free. Not sure I would delve head first into eating fried bugs, but the challenge would be there if I desired.

Before Europe, we worked every single day. It wasn't until I got back that we started a new rotation of forty-eight hours on, twenty-four hours off. Today is my first day off.

While I was gone to Europe, Taji took incoming on the airfield and hit one of the Iraqi birds (helicopters). Three contractors were working on the helicopter at the time and they were hit by shrapnel.

For the last three nights, I've heard IEDs and car bombs going off. I can hear them off base and the explosions cause my door to slam with each explosion. Sometimes, we'll hear three in a row. Whoomp! Whoomp! Whoomp!

The other night when I was in dispatch, I heard the siren go off and the "big voice" said, "Incoming. Incoming. Incoming." We went to the bunkers but didn't hear an explosion. I called BDOC (Base Defense Operating Center) to see if it was a test and it wasn't, but we never got word as to what happened. Maybe a mortar came onto base and didn't detonate.

Chapter 17

Have I Lost My Mind?

It's ten minutes until morning briefing.

"What are you looking for?" one of the guys asks.

"Nothing," I reply with a slight irritation in my tone.

I pace around the firehouse, frustrated and confused.

"Hey, Lizzy, Chief wants to talk to you. I think he's mad."

"What? What did I do wrong?" I ask.

I head out to the app bay to see the assistant chief leaning against the engine with his arms crossed. "You missing something?"

"Yeah," I reply.

Chief pulls my radio out from under his arm. "I found this outside last night. This is a high security risk. You can lose your job over these mistakes."

I can see he's disappointed by his body language, but his tone softens as he speaks to me. It's as if he's angry but can't stay mad.

"I'm so sorry. We were doing sprints last night and I don't even remember setting it down. I know it's supposed to be with me at all times."

"Well, don't let it happen again. I'ma keep this between us this time. Okay?" He looks at me with a serious expression.

Chief has been like a mentor and friend to me. I know he'll always look out for my best interest and it's nice to know someone has my back.

"Thank you, Chief." I head into the training room for morning briefing.

The crazy thing is I don't really feel right. It feels like I've just lost my mind. I don't know how I could be so stupid to just leave my radio out where anyone could grab it.

I've been back at my base for a couple of weeks now and Alex is also back in Iraq. It's my day off again, so I get online and talk to him.

"I feel so strange today. I feel confused and anxious. My body chemistry must be out of whack for some reason."

"Have you started?" Alex asks me.

I realize he's referring to my menstrual cycle. "I haven't, but I know I'll start any day because I feel a lot of cramping. There's no way I'm pregnant."

"When are you supposed to start?"

"Well, I was supposed to start on Monday, so I'm like four days late, but I'll probably start at any time."

Alex's prodding strikes my curiosity. I type a question into my Internet browser. "Can you feel like you're going to start your period if you're pregnant?"

The response: "Yes, it's common to feel cramping similar to PMS during your first trimester of pregnancy."

I cover my mouth in shock to this response. I could be pregnant!

I walk a half mile to the PX and purchase a pregnancy test. When I get back home, I sneak into my bathroom and take it right away. In an instant, the result comes up positive. How weird! My natural response is to feel excited, even though I realize it's the result of being irresponsible. I can't help but smile.

It's my turn to be in dispatch, so for twelve hours a day I sit in a chair, in a little room, and wait for emergency phone calls. If I get a call, I have to dispatch the appropriate resources to the scene. I've already been in here for a week now. Seven days of twelve hours, sitting in a chair is exhausting. We've had a couple of emergency calls, but nothing big has really happened.

I start dispatch at 0800 (8:00 a.m.), and then I'm off dispatch at 2000 (8:00 p.m.). From 2000 all through the night until 0800, I'm assigned to the fire engine. So I'm working twenty-four hours around the clock, but two different duties.

Right now, I'm assigned to the fire engine for the next two hours. I drag my sleepy head out of bed and jump in the shower to freshen up for my day. I'm so sleepy. The warm water is pouring down my back and it feels refreshing as I tip my head backward into the water.

The house tones go off. From inside my watery cave I hear my portable radio emit an emergency traffic message.

The gentle ambiance of a steamy shower has changed into an urgent "Hurry your ass up and get out the door" procedure.

I leap out of my shower and initiate a speedy towel pat-down. I omit underwear and a bra as I wiggle into my khakis, T-shirt, and Crocs. In one smooth motion, I grab a hair tie with one hand while opening the door with the other.

I lunge toward the exit door and hear the engine running in the apparatus bay. The door doesn't open, so I try again.

I shout out in discouragement, "The door is locked!"

I sprint down the hallway toward the middle exit and surge toward the engine. The engine begins to pull away and then it pauses for me to leap in.

"Thanks!" I say to the driver as we take off.

I throw on my bunker gear to cover up the inappropriateness of my commando boobs, being that there was no time to waste with undergarments. I pull my dripping wet dreadlocks up into a quick ponytail and plop back into my seat with a big sigh.

My partner looks at me and smiles. "Nice job," he says.

I smile back, feeling relieved yet irritated that I almost missed a call due to a door being locked or jammed.

This is a medical call. We arrive to a housing unit where three contractors are standing outside, waving us over frantically. These contractors are from a country somewhere in Europe.

I walk in to see our patient lying on the floor, conscious and shaking with bloody vomit on his face. The paramedics are on their way, and this clearly looks like a situation where our patient needs a greater level of care.

Fire Diary

We try to ask the man questions, but he cannot respond to us. His pupils are dilated and nonreactive to light. This doesn't look good.

"I wonder if he was *inhaling*," my partner remarks. "A lot of guys over here get bored and start experimenting with those air canisters."

It's an interesting thought, but we can't find any evidence of that. The guys that were with him have no information for us.

We load him up for the medics and have little information to pass on to them. We probably won't receive further updates on his status either. I always wonder how things turn out after a call.

We head back to the station and I have to get ready for another twelve-hour shift in dispatch. I wonder what would've happened if we had a fire call. I'm paranoid about the health of my baby if my body is subjected to that kind of stress. I want this baby to be healthy and strong and I'm worried about the heat and intense physical conditions causing a miscarriage. And I'm a firefighter in Iraq! Now what?

So I'm faced with a major decision. Do I go home, or do I stay? When should I go home? If I stay, am I going to be afraid to do my job due to fears of miscarriage or harm to the baby?

It's strange how Taji feels like home—very strange. I'm just going to have to take it week by week.

Alex and I are having a really good night talking on Skype. We're both watching Harry Potter on the AFN movie channel (Air Forces Network) and searching for baby names—boy names specifically, since we already have a girl name picked out. I fell in love with the name Yasmine *(Yaz-meen)*. It's the Persian name that was given to my friend Vanessa as her false identity for her duties as an interrogator.

While typing on Skype to Alex, he tells me how excited he is to be a daddy. I'm excited too! It's just awesome to think that since I'm five weeks along, our baby is the size of a sesame seed and its heart will start beating this week. Amazing!

My symptoms today have been the same as the last couple of days. I get really overheated and sweaty. By the time I get into the

DFAC, I feel like I'm having a hot flash. The soldiers ask me, "Are you all right?" as I fan myself with my hand and get a little out of breath. The summer heat has subsided, so that's no longer a good excuse.

My morning sickness has come on full force as well, and I really need a good breakfast to help ease the nausea. I'm having strong cramping in my lower back, but it's all exciting because I know what's happening inside my body right now.

Chapter 18

A Mortar

It's Thanksgiving and I'm having a difficult time being happy. Alex hasn't been talking to me the last couple of days. He says he's really busy at work, but my intuitions tell me something's not right. He's acting distanced and I'm not sure why. Is he afraid? My mind is full of questions. Why won't he talk to me anymore? Why is he short and apathetic when I do get ahold of him? I realize the death of his father is still fresh. When in Europe, he seemed to lack a certain light in his eyes, like a piece of him was gone inside. I understand healing takes time and can ultimately reshape the person who is hurting, but I want to be there to support him. I'm scared, really scared.

So anyways, it's Thanksgiving and it's also my day off. I didn't know the DFAC stopped serving breakfast early on holidays. I'm already off to a rough start because I didn't get to eat. Breakfast has been the only cure for my morning sickness. I get nauseous every morning and hold back the desire to vomit. I need a good meal to keep me from my misery.

By lunchtime, I've felt sick all day and I'm hoping to get a good Thanksgiving lunch in my stomach. Maybe it will lift my mood too. I'm down in the dumps with a knot in my throat as I'm just trying to hold back tears. I wish I was working because I'm not easily distracting myself from the negative thoughts and fears.

A new unit from the army arrived on base two weeks ago and the unit they're replacing hasn't left yet, so our only DFAC is over packed. The line is wrapped around the gate, and I don't have the energy to stand for that long. A lot of the other firefighters opted not to eat lunch at all. No turkey for me. I guess I'll scrounge through my closet and see if I can get some peanut butter and bread.

This is pathetic. I'm totally feeling sorry for myself today and I can't seem to kick it. I suppose it gives me a perspective on people who are less fortunate. I'm just thankful to have a wonderful family, I'm thankful that I live here with a great group of guys who treat me like their sister, and I'm thankful to have a beautiful blessing transforming in my belly.

The time now is 1600 (4:00 p.m.) and I'm in my room, feeling down. A loud, aggressive knock thunders over my door.

"Head to the bunkers!" Chief hollers out to me.

I'm in my pajama pants and the usual Taji Fire Department T-shirt and slip on a pair of Crocs. I open my door and walk pragmatically to the bunker. I'm last to arrive and greeted by twenty of my colleagues squished into a dusty and dark eight-foot by eight-foot cave.

So what happens when you cram a bunch of boys into a tight space? Of course, somebody farts as loud as they can. The humorous part on their behalf is that we have a choice between two evils: smelling a nasty man-made gas cloud or risk getting hit by a mortar. He actually got me to crack a smile with his mischievous mission. We all hang tight in the bunkers.

Dispatch comes across the radio with an announcement. There's an MCI (mass casualty incident) at Pod 34.

The engine crew exits the bunkers and dashes to their apparatus. Since it's my day off, I'm not allowed to leave the bunker until the all-clear has been reported.

The engine crew arrives on scene, and the two victims have already been expedited to the army medical clinic by their own cohorts. The mortar went through the roof of a CHU and was occupied by two soldiers.

From the little information we receive, it sounds like the victims' wounds are not life threatening. They were hit by shrapnel from flying debris as the mortar entered but did not detonate. I'm thankful for that and pray they will be okay.

So I'm sitting in the bunker, on a Kevlar vest, in the dirt, thinking, *Okay, I'm pregnant in Iraq on Thanksgiving, hiding in a bunker. Nice.* To top it off, there's a hole in the crotch of my new pajama pants that I just got in Dubai. I just noticed this—don't know if anyone else saw it. Hopefully not, but do I really care right now? No, I guess not.

I realize I have a lot of decisions to make surrounding this pregnancy. We all want to go home, but it's difficult since I've been caught calling this place "home" on occasion. I would also really miss my Taji family. If I go home, I don't know where I'm going and which friends will still be there for me. On top of that, I feel safe here. Try to figure that one out.

Once we receive the all-clear from base defense, I put on my workout clothes and force myself to stay in the routine of exercise. I walk to the gym and watch the neon-orange sun set off into the distant layer of desert sand. The sand floats in an even layer, high above land, and is topped with blue sky. I find a love for nature's beauty in this otherwise moment of indifference.

There are two Blackhawks in the distance, hovering over Pod 34 as investigations and inspections continue. Our engine has left the scene and EOD (the explosive ordinance disposal team) has command over removal of UXO (unexploded ordinance).

After the gym, I finally get a meal at the DFAC. There's leftover Thanksgiving food from lunchtime and I'm just happy to eat a decent meal. After someone on base is sent away with shrapnel wounds, I really shouldn't be complaining about my morning sickness and relationship issues.

Alex finally breaks his silence to tell me the relationship is over. He doesn't give me much of a reason and I'm extremely confused right now. Regardless, the pain of rejection is agonizing. I'm so angry and disappointed. My heart is so heavy and it aches. It feels as if my heart has been replaced with a ten-pound brick. I'm in too much shock to react or cry. I try to tell myself it's just because we don't really know each other and we rushed things, but the Devil is in my ear telling me it's because I'm not good enough and I'm not attractive. I feel the downward spiral pulling me in and I need to stop myself from falling.

Wait a minute. This is not what I envisioned for myself: being a single mom. Besides, I still believe in the vision I had over a year ago that gave me hope amid my depression and desire for life to end. I know what I saw and I know that it will come true. I was so happy in that moment with that beautiful little girl, but I suppose I didn't see a man in that moment, and there was no indication if there was one around at all. I know I'm wrong for being intimate with a man I'm not married to, but this is acceptable in our culture, right? I suppose I still know I was wrong, and I shouldn't let a cultural "norm" guide my personal decisions. Either way, I feel so blessed to have life inside me and I'm going to choose to stay positive and ask God for forgiveness and guidance.

Vanessa and Janisse are leaving the base soon, as are many of the soldiers. Although many of my original fire brothers have left the base, many new firefighters have joined our firehouse. Little by little, we've gained one new firefighter at a time. I'm so happy that all the new people have great personalities and have fit in right away. I remember when I was the "new guy." It doesn't take long to gain seniority around here.

We all have call signs so that we can refer to each other over the radio without risking our security. My call name is Care Bear. With all the new folks at the station, we have to create nicknames for them. It's not always easy making up names. One day, we were all playing basketball and one of the new guys showed up to play in shorts and tan combat boots. I nick named him Boots and it stuck. Boots is one of my good friends, as are many of the other new guys who've arrived.

I'm almost at the end of my first trimester of pregnancy and many of my closer friends at the station know that I'm pregnant. They know I'm trying to be strong although it appears I will be venturing into motherhood alone. Here I go again out on my own. I've also consoled with my captains and chiefs here about the pregnancy. They're willing to keep it undisclosed for the time being. They know I will have to go home soon anyways. They're letting me decide when it's time. I appreciate the autonomy they've allowed me in this situation. I did, however, agree that I would no longer run calls. I will strictly be working twelve-hour days in dispatch. Ugh! That's twelve long hours to sit and think, and think, and think. Some of the guys will occasionally drop in to chat and keep me company, so I'm never really lonely. I appreciate that.

I've only drunk two ounces of coffee in almost a month. I used to not go a day without it. I woke up one morning when I was six weeks pregnant and suddenly had an aversion to coffee, chocolate, and red meat. Many smells have become too strong for me to tolerate, so I hold my breath and plug my nose a lot. Since I'm in dispatch all day, I have to have my meals brought to me. I feel a little like a diva making requests for certain foods and requests not to even see other foods cross my path. It's not in my personality to be so demanding and picky, but this is just another interesting change due to the hormones. I'm fascinated by it actually—the power that hormones have over us.

My only pregnancy craving is for citric and sweet foods. I tell Gilbert and Boots about my strong desire for Skittles, but I can't go to the PX to buy some because I'm stuck in dispatch all day. I'll definitely go buy some after work.

Later in the day, Gilbert and Boots swagger into my dispatch room. They have big, menacing grins on their smug faces as they pop handfuls of Skittles teasingly into their mouths. After they're satisfied, dangling my craving in front of me, they hand over a large, red bag of Skittles to me. Ahh, how sweet!

"Thank you sooo much!" I give them both big hugs.

Other than citric foods, I'm craving a good ol' turkey and cheese deli sandwich. Not because I'm pregnant though, just because the sandwiches in Iraq are horrible. The bread is dry, and the cheese, meat, and condiments are just not nearly as satisfying.

It's Janisse's and Vanessa's last week here. Vanessa is able to come visit me to say good-bye. We're both in a time of deep thought with so much of the future unknown. She's returning to the States, which is a big transition from being over here. We sit outside station 2 on rickety lawn chairs in the clay-colored and hardened desert mud. She leans back in the chair and relaxes while rays of sun peek through the trees. She has her army uniform on and her M4 rifle resting across her chest.

The weather is perfect outside: sunny and not too hot. We sit in silence, just relaxing and enjoying the comfortable temperature. I'm immersed in thoughts of my decisions ahead. I stare out at the deep tire imprints, semi-permanent divots left from vehicles driving through the mud on rainy days.

Vanessa knows that I've chosen to name my daughter Yasmine, if in fact I have a little girl. Out of her pocket, she pulls out the Velcro nameplate that she wore throughout her tour of Iraq as an interrogator. The name says, "Yasmine." I smile and give her a big hug. "Thank you!" I say to her with so much gratitude in my heart. I hug her gently as my breasts have changed from pregnancy and they are severely painful to any pressure. I learned that hugs hurt because some of my buddies would greet me with a big, hearty hug before they knew how much it hurt me.

Working in dispatch means I can't leave my radio or the phone lines. Well, obviously I'll need a moment here and there to step aside and use the restroom. Since I'm pregnant, I have to pee more often than normal. Because I'm still responsible for all emergency-radio traffic during these moments, there is a conveniently placed Porta-John right outside my dispatch room. What an awesome way to spend the first trimester of my pregnancy—hovering over everyone else's filth. As displeasing as it may be, I have to laugh at the humbling experience. I count it as character building.

I have a horrible headache right now and I'm nauseous. I cried a lot today. It was just a struggle to stay positive and I don't know what to do. I want to go home so badly, but I feel this is a struggle I'm supposed to go through for some reason. I also just don't feel ready to go home. It's confusing when you feel strong about two complete opposite decisions.

I just heard a new sound outside. It's not a mortar. It's not a helicopter. It's raining! For the first time in the seven months I've been in the desert, it's raining. My shift is over and I have to step outside to observe the occasion with some of the other guys.

Afterward, a few of us come back in and hang out in one of their rooms, which was my first room here. I love my Taji brothers. We sit in this tiny room in our pajamas and Crocs, talking and laughing. They all know I'm pregnant and that my relationship didn't exactly go through the way one would hope. I'm thankful they aren't being judgmental of my situation. They comfort me and make things easier to handle. They've also been a great support group for me, listening to the ups and downs when I need to talk. I don't have girlfriends on base now that Janisse and Vanessa are gone, but these guys have been just as good as girlfriends to me.

Chapter 19
Christmas in Iraq

DEPLETED URANIUM. THIS IS WHAT I think when I pass the bone yard. *Radiation.* This is what I think of when we do training on the airfield near the Apaches. Carcinogenic products of combustion. There's a constant black cloud of poisonous gases burning outside our base almost daily. Along with these products, there's the small detail of IDF entering our base on occasion. My body is no longer my own. I can no longer live the same carefree life I've subjected myself to. Everything seems like a potential hazard to my unborn child right now. I can't even look at the mounds of pigeon poop on the app bay floor without thinking of the potential viruses one could conceive. I can't wear a dust mask or hold my breath forever!

The dust has been shaken from the polyvinyl needles of the Christmas tree and it's placed out on a stand for the season. For a short time, there was rain and temperatures in the fifties and sixties. Now the sky is clear blue and it's warmed up a bit. As someone from the great Northwest, I would not have suspected that it was Christmas season unless the calendar told me so.

I wasn't aware that there was a little chapel near the firehouse, and some of the new guys invited me to join in on a church service.

A group of us head over to the chapel after I'm off dispatch for the evening. We're a little late because they had to wait for me. Oops!

"Thanks for waiting, guys," I say.

"No problem," they reply.

I'm feeling very content today knowing that my baby is growing and already has a beating heart. What an amazing feeling!

The five of us shuffle over the gravel and sand until we arrive to the chapel. We're greeted with nods and smiles from the military servicemen and women and take a seat in the pews.

There are screens at the front of the room with lyrics as we sing karaoke-style Christmas music. I'll admit I would've found this kind of dorky previously, but I'm happy to be here with my new friends, singing all the fun Christmas music of my youth. Although the baby inside me is smaller than a peanut, I feel like I'm sharing this moment with someone very special. I'm happy and can't stop smiling.

When we return to the station, all of our firefighters from both firehouses congregate in the day room for name drawing. For Christmas, we will each draw a name of someone to buy a present for. We then will spend around ten dollars for that person. This is a fun idea even though we realize most of us will be shopping with a limited selection at the PX.

It's Christmas Eve. Tomorrow is my last full day here at Taji, and then I will spend a few days in Baghdad. I'm kind of nervous. I don't know what the future holds. I've kept my family up to date on my news. I told them right away when I discovered I was pregnant. They were disappointed, but they realize I'm an adult and should be capable of making appropriate decisions for my life. My stepmom so sweetly apologized that they were unable to give me the excited response to my big news, due to the unexpectedness of it. When I broke the news to them, there was dead silence for a long period of time. That's actually what I had expected, so I was mentally prepared for almost any reaction.

I told my chief I was ready to go home. We knew he would have to communicate with headquarters to get the arrangements made.

We also knew I would be sent home immediately once they were made aware of my circumstance.

Once headquarters was made aware, they helped arrange my flights home. They were also very kind to me, offering me the opportunity to come back and work for them again in the future if I chose. I know this won't be an option; I will be a mother and my baby will need me.

I cannot go back to my job at home in Washington until June, and now I'm not sure if I can go back at all because of my pregnancy. I need to say my prayers for guidance. Also, Alex still won't communicate with me. He's hurt me deeply and now I'm just trying to stay strong and push myself away from him emotionally.

I'm now mentally preparing myself to become a single mom. It's crazy how fast life can change. I've been sad at moments and almost start to feel down, but I'm determined not to let myself. I refuse to. I don't know where my life is going, but I can only stay hopeful and hold on to faith. I have faith.

I'm already sad to leave my Taji brothers. These guys have been so great to live and work with. They've been supportive and caring. It's safe to say I'm nervous about leaving what has oddly become my home.

It's Christmas Day and it's also my very last day here at Taji Fire Department. I'm coming to the end of my first trimester and really want to go home to see a doctor. I want my little baby to be healthy and I don't know anything about being pregnant.

All of our firefighters are here at station 1 preparing for the barbecue and gift exchange. This will be the last time I'll get to see everyone together. I'm excited to go home, and sad to leave. I'm looking forward to one more trip to Baghdad and one more stay in Dubai. I'm gonna miss traveling through these areas.

As suspected, many of the gifts were purchased from the PX, but people are surprisingly creative, regardless of the limitations. I receive the best gift of all: a tennis racquet bug zapper. Everyone wants to try it out, and one of the guys volunteers to try out the effects of the racquet on himself.

Everyone in the dayroom is quiet and watches as he holds out his little pinky. I encourage him to stay still as I place the racquet on his finger. As soon as he touches the wires in the racquet, he jumps back from the zap of electricity and we all laugh at our immature curiosity.

Although I love my gift, I know I'm leaving tomorrow morning and the guys will appreciate it much more if I just leave it in their care.

I told my family not to send anything since I'll be home in less than a week.

After we open presents, I receive a large brown box in the mail. I open the box to find cards and Christmas decorations and gifts. I pick up the card lying on the very top; it's signed with love from the Mountain View Church Choir. I feel so surprised and my heart is happy. If they only could know how much this means to me, how much I want to feel cared for at this moment.

During my last few days in Baghdad, I'm able to say good-bye to all those who I've met along the way. Being that this is my fourth time staying here, I've also made friends with random people in passing. Most of them I don't know by name, but I know their faces. While en route to the DFAC and PX, I stop and chat with my friendly acquaintances. I share my pregnancy news with them and they congratulate and warmly wish me the best.

There's no need to tell the firefighters; they already know. Telephone, telethon, tell a fireman. I visit the firehouse and join them for lunch at the DFAC. It's great to see them again. After all the training we did in Texas, it doesn't seem as if time has passed since we were last together.

As expected, the siren overhead prompts us to head to the nearest bunker as the base takes incoming. Hopefully, this will be the last time I ever have to hide in a bunker to evade flying mortars.

Chapter 20

Coming Home for Good

I GAZE UP AT RANDOM BULLET holes on the cream-colored exterior. I wonder how many more there were when the war began. If I were in a US airport right now, I would hear the announcement. "Do not leave your luggage unattended at any time." I'm apprehensive at the thought of leaving my baggage here at Baghdad International Airport in a makeshift, cement tunnel.

I stand among fifty confused US civilians divided into three single-file lines. We do as we're told and leave our luggage behind. The Iraqis direct us out of the dreary, T-wall tunnel and release the K9s to sniff-search our baggage. They pat down each individual.

A man points at me then gestures to a nearby door where an Iraqi woman sits. The woman wearing a headscarf peers out and waves me over. Although it's typical for a female to conduct physical security checks on another female, this is the first airport where I'm completely out of sight from the men while being searched. I'm nervous about the seclusion from my group. I creep into a stifling, cordoned-off room while everyone else stays outside. Two women pat me down then wave me off with a warm smile.

This is my last time leaving Baghdad International Airport. I didn't have to go through all of these extra security steps while passing through two months earlier. This minor inconvenience is only the beginning of a long journey ahead.

I tread over the white-tiled flooring of the expansive yet empty foyer to retrieve my flight ticket to Dubai. The handsome, hazel-eyed man at the ticket counter was the same man I saw several months earlier while arriving in the country. He was the one who handed me my Iraqi visa and I remember my attempts to avoid eye contact with him. Back then, I was trying not to stare at him. He gave me more than a glance as well.

I walk up to the counter and smile at him shyly.

His eyes meet mine. "You are beautiful," he comments unexpectedly.

"You are too!" I pipe back without thinking.

He hands me my ticket and I scurry away while debating in my mind whether or not that was a culturally acceptable response.

I appreciate the flattery at this moment, as I am now happily pregnant but unexpectedly single and unsure of what is to come. There are a lot of unknowns to handle in my near and distant future. And let's not forget that I'm also recovering from that horrible haircut from my last stay in Dubai.

The flight from Baghdad to the United Arab Emirates wasn't too bad. It wasn't until I caught my flight from Dubai to London that my morning nausea turned into sporadic vomiting and several unanticipated trips to the bathroom. I'm at the end of my first trimester now and have experienced plenty of morning nausea, but this is the first time I've actually produced something from it. I decide to keep a paper receptacle close by for the remaining trek as I continue westbound to the other side of the globe.

Bittersweet emotions are at a pinnacle as I reflect on my recent adventures. Over just a few short years, I've sustained an intimate encounter with life in ways that make me feel as if a decade has passed. Depression, death, trauma, religion, travel, culture, war, peace, rejection, life, and love. As a young and somewhat naïve woman from small-town USA, I didn't anticipate that I would've acquainted with topics of such magnitude. I'm feeling challenged from more recent events and any pain that I feel is a miraculous motivation to my soul. I feel hopeful and I'm going to choose to keep my head up.

It's been a crazy transition back to society and life. I'm beginning to understand why some people actually prefer to be in Iraq instead of facing reality back in the real world. We crave options and freedom and opportunity, but there's simplicity that comes along with life on a military base. You know where you're going to eat every day. You know what options you will be given for food and beverage. You know what you will wear, how you will do your hair, where you will go shopping, and who you will spend your time with.

I realize how complex we make our lives at home sometimes. I've been away from home for over seven months and already I'm behind on the latest trends. If I called myself a tomboy before, I'm more so now than ever and suddenly feel the pressure to step up and fit into society's expectations of beauty. For this reason, I notice that I'm wearing more makeup lately to compensate for my lack of esteem. The more self-conscious I am, the darker my lipstick and eyeliner become. Yes, you now know my secret.

Being away from home created an illusion that is consistent with the old sayings "Out of sight, out of mind" and "Ignorance is bliss." I didn't have to worry about what was going on at home unless my family called to tell me.

Although there's much to do and a lot on my to-do list, I feel thankful for my recent opportunities. In a short amount of time, I've seen and learned more about the world and about my country and military than I ever could have by staying in place. This was hands down the most eye-opening adventure of my life. I don't feel I have time to sit back and reminisce on my experiences now because there's a metaphorical fog surrounding me. I need to focus on navigating past the obstacles of uncertainty and the mires of potential destruction. Staying positive now and growing in my relationship with God is my greatest endeavor at this moment.

My renters are expecting to stay in my home for a few more months, and I want to return to work in a few months. That's right: I'm a firefighter and I'm still pregnant, but I want to return to my job. In this economy, as a single mom, I need to look out for my child's best interest. I don't know God's plan, but my current fears lead me to believe that I need to reconstitute my old life to secure our future.

Since my house is occupied and I don't begin work again for a while, my parents have allowed me to live with them. Their home is three hours away from my house, but I'm thankful for the opportunity to come home from my journey and take this time to grow closer to them.

I hadn't spent as much time with my family over the last few years and feel thankful to have a reason to be near them more often. I'm going to take full advantage of this time to reconnect with the people most important in my life.

Meanwhile, I'm going to do everything I can to stay committed to my return to duty as a firefighter. I registered at the community college for courses in fire science and biology so that I can keep my mind and body active in fire and emergency medicine. I also started volunteering at the hospital so that I can get out of the house and be around people. I've scheduled several trips up to my firehouse for trainings and visitations with old friends and members of my church choir. I'm determined to move forward.

I'm at the doctor's office for my very first appointment. Other than the pregnancy test I took over in Iraq, I haven't taken any other tests to confirm my pregnancy. What if I'm not really pregnant? What if all those symptoms were just coincidence? I've traveled all the way around the world for this appointment and I feel so nervous.

The doctor has me lie on the table. She has a hand-held monitor and she's lubing up the device that she will rub on my belly to see the baby. I become nervous and want to creep away from the device. What if there's no baby in my tummy at all? I'd be afraid to make this discovery after everything I've been through.

She places the lubricated wand on my lower abdomen and it feels cold and wet as she rolls it around. I begin to hear a pounding heartbeat, and on the black and white monitor, I see what looks like a jumping peanut. I can clearly see the big chunk that is the head and the big chunk that is the rest of the body. The peanut is bouncing around and wiggling nonstop. I begin laughing so hard that we lose view of my little baby. I want to keep watching my bouncing peanut, but I can't stop my nervous, excited laughter. "That's my baby!"

I found out I was denied unemployment; I don't have insurance, a job, or income; and I'm living in my hometown with my parents. This is me, momentarily acknowledging the "fog" that I previously mentioned as my current situation.

Every day, I start out with a long to-do list and a positive outlook for my future. With every attempt I make to achieve something great, the amount of negative outcomes stack up against me. I don't want to become discouraged and I don't want to stop trying. I feel like this is just another trial that I need to go through.

After speaking with my employer, I get a strong impression that I'm not going to get me my job back. I can understand this isn't a normal situation and almost don't expect that I will be reinstated. At this point, I'm not feeling successful in this endeavor, but the lack of a direct response is muddying up the water. I guess I will have to stay persistent and professional until I know that I've done everything I can.

Okay, on to the next item of business. If I don't get my job back, how will I pay for the mortgage? Maybe I can lower my monthly payments.

I call my mortgage loan company. Yet again, more bad news. I can't refinance my house because I don't have a job, and if I did, the loan would cost more and my monthly payment would actually be more.

The man on the line tells me about the hardship program. The process would ruin my credit just to apply and they may not even accept my request. The simple fact that I would need to recognize that my current situation is considered a "hardship" is pure disappointment.

I hang up the phone and again feel devastated. I lose my strength and positive spirit into a messy sob. My bill for my doctor's appointment was just around $1,000 because I don't have insurance.

Baby on the way, boyfriend left me, no job, no income, and a house upside down over forty grand. Beautiful! What am I going to do now? What am I going to do?

The only thing keeping me going right now is the memory of the vision I received that one night over a year ago: the vision of my daughter and how happy I was in that moment. I can't see my path through this fog, but I know it picks up beyond this discomfort into something beautiful and amazing.

I went to bed depressed and then woke up feeling just as bad. A new day should bring me relief and rejuvenation but it hasn't today. I'm watching the news with my dad, trying to stay calm and relaxed. I take a bite of my crispy toast. Mid crunch, I burst into a full-blown sob. With a chunk of dry toast in my mouth, I try to stop the tears and emotions but they rush out of me like a geyser.

My dad, not expecting this random outcry, comes to my side and pats my hair to comfort me. "Honey, I'm surprised you've held it together so well for this long. It's going to be okay."

My parents actually expected more emotions from me to begin with. Because I've been trying to be so strong, they felt I wasn't taking my situation seriously. I am taking this seriously, and that's why I need to be so strong.

I'm blessed to have such a great family and I appreciate them so much.

This is an incredibly humbling experience. I can't point the finger at everyone around me for everything wrong. I need to put my pride aside and reflect. I can see in hindsight how my decisions have gotten me to where I am now. There are so many things going on right now that my brain doesn't even know which one to focus on. It hurts, but I need to remember this feeling so that I make better choices, and also so I don't make others feel the way I do right now. I haven't always been good to others; maybe this is a good lesson. Now I know what it feels like to be emotionally torn down and cast away like I don't matter. Humbling, very humbling. I need to know what this feels like, for perspective. I can acknowledge the positive lesson in this moment.

During this season of continuous disappointments, I simultaneously experience nuances of invigoration. Whenever I recover from a negative blow, I just want to stand up, dust off, and move forward again. It's as if I'm getting knocked down over and over again, but my passion to come out on top drives me. They always say you have to have "thick skin" to be a firefighter, but I've never felt as tenacious about life as I do at this juncture. Although I break down and cry on occasion, I feel strong and I keep trying to figure out what it is I have to do. This makes the positive moments more meaningful.

Now I'm enquiring with my Realtor about a short sale and I'm thinking about stopping my payment on the house next month. If I don't get a job, I'll probably lose the house anyways. I don't know if I will receive unemployment, after I challenge their initial decision, and I want to save the money I have for the baby: diapers, formula—all that stuff. Gas is now up to $3.60 a gallon and the economy is looking grim. I lived pretty tight on money before, almost paycheck to paycheck as most Americans do, but with zero income, it's pretty scary.

My Realtor is going to work with me to try a short sale on the house. We're looking at putting it up for sale for about $46,000 less than is owed on the home. Since the economy has taken a downturn, my home has devalued over and over again. With a short sale, some lenders will forgive the balance due and some will come after you for the difference. I'm hoping for the forgiveness of the balance obviously, because I'm not in a position to keep paying on this house.

Big news! I finally qualify for unemployment. It took hiring a lawyer to get it, but I achieved it. There's more good news; after several phone calls over a three-month period, I've finally been accepted for COBRA insurance. With my unemployment money, I can pay for my insurance, and now my doctor's bills won't be as expensive. I can have my regular visits to make sure my baby is growing healthy and strong. What a blessing!

Also, Alex and I have had a few short conversations. This whole situation is awkward; we're not ready to discuss our pending parental partnership and neither of us knows what we're doing. I'm too prideful to ask for help, but he realizes my doctor's bills are adding up. He told me he would help me out. I'm feeling extremely thankful right now.

Chapter 21

What Does the Future Hold?

TODAY MY FAMILY ACCOMPANIED ME to a very special ultrasound. We found out that I'm having a baby girl. Although I've never wavered on my belief that I would have a little girl in my life, this just further confirmed to me that God is fulfilling the beautiful gift that he has shown to me. Because I was single when I saw the vision of my daughter, I honestly couldn't tell what ethnicity she was. She reminded me of my little cousin who was adopted from Korea. I now know her ethnicity is part Hispanic, and I believe with all my heart that this is her.

Her movements inside my tummy are getting bigger. I used to feel only a tiny touch or hiccup, but now I can feel her elbows and legs squirming around. I love being pregnant! And I'm so in love with this little baby inside me.

I'm no less excited about my baby than if I were with Alex, but this is definitely an experience that should be shared with someone special. I've never been pregnant before so I didn't know what to expect with my emotions and physical changes to my body. I keep myself composed and repress my emotions and negative thoughts on the situation as best as I can. On occasion, like last night, I find myself sobbing from the realization that I'm a single mom and I don't have someone here to feel my baby kick and move. I want him to be here to kiss my tummy and love this unborn baby as much as I do.

I've caught myself playing over and over in my mind the hardships and grief of the recent events in my life. I have to stop myself and allow the hurt and rejection to leave my mind. There's no reason to replay the things that have been done. With some of the situations that have been difficult, I've been guided to evaluate and learn from, but not continue into a battle. I've always liked the saying "Choose your battles," but it can be difficult to do when you're under pressure and you just want to fight back against it all.

You know how you can go along in life and learn little things here and there? It's exciting when you have those moments where you learn about life. Not book smarts and not even street smarts, but when you realize that you've gained a nugget of some real life perspective that hits you like that "light bulb moment." You are forever changed by whatever thought or perspective that almost indescribably adds wisdom to your life. Sometimes, those moments are few and far between. Sometimes, they come in the middle of the night when you're distressed and can't sleep. Sometimes, you're feeling lonely and depressed or crying. Those moments are so powerful that they can almost immediately draw you upward from the downward fall you were experiencing only a second earlier. I'm amorous about life right now because I'm being pushed and pulled and challenged mentally in all different ways and so many outward-appearing negative events are creating these moments for me over and over again. I look like a train wreck to the onlooker, but these events are so powerful and my adventure is pretty awesome for the lessons learned and wisdom gained.

I heard from the guys at my base in Taji that they got hit fifty-one times yesterday morning by IDF (indirect fire). I'm thankful none of them are hurt and I can't imagine what it would be like if that had happened while I was pregnant on base.

I feel as if my hormones are in full force now. My joints are loose, my body aches, and I'm emotional and depressed. But everything else is going well. I recognize this is just part of being pregnant.

My nephews and niece have been so excited about their cousin growing in my belly. My youngest nephew likes to give her hugs in my belly and he'll put his ear on my tummy to listen for sounds.

"I think I hear her crying," he'll say. "How is she lying in your tummy? What does she eat? What is she doing right now?" He's always curious about every detail of her fetal life.

He's been asking me a lot of questions about her, so I let him come to my ultrasound, along with my mom and stepdad.

Baby Yasmine sleeps during the thirty-two-week ultrasound. No leg or arm movements. She just moves her lips around and squishes her cheeks. Her heartbeat sounds great and all of her growth is within the normal range. She weighs four pounds now and should gain about a half a pound per week. I keep wondering if she's going to be here on her due date, or sooner, or later. There are only eight to ten more weeks.

Yasmine suddenly waves her hand in front of the monitor. "She waved at me!" my mom exclaims. "She said hi to her grammy!"

I'm happy to see my mom excited. I know it was rough at first when I first broke the news of my pregnancy. Regardless, my family has gathered behind me, loved me, and supported me during the journey so far. My mom wants to be there with me when I give birth to her granddaughter.

My symptoms have been a little more intense in the last few weeks, but they vary from day to day. I suffer massive heartburn and chow down Tums like candy. I also get really weak and out of breath easily. At night, I usually have to pee really badly and I'll end up waking up at about 3:00 a.m. and not being able to go back to sleep for an hour or two.

I used to think I wanted to have a natural birth with no drugs or epidural. I said I would hold out as long as I could and try not to accept any type of assistance. Now that I'm thirty-two weeks pregnant, I've already given up on that idea and think that I want the epidural. I keep seeing videos of women in labor and the pain and challenges they have. I always thought I would be able to handle the challenge of severe pain associated with childbirth, but at this point, I'm already so emotionally vulnerable that I don't want to have extra physical challenges if I don't have to. I won't have the dad by my side, and now that I'm battling to keep my job, I don't even know where I'll be living at the time. There's a possibility I could become emotionally stressed and sad. I want to be as positive and happy as possible because I'm so excited to meet my baby girl and I want to enjoy those first moments with her as much as possible. So it looks like I didn't hold out as long as I thought I would for the pain meds.

My stepmom has been coming with me to my birthing classes and I've really appreciated her presence. At the beginning of the class, we all had to introduce ourselves. There were seven couples and one other girl who came with her mom. That mom made sure we knew that her daughter had a man and that she was just filling in. She announced it so that no one would mistake her legitimacy and I found myself irritated with her need to establish that with us. At moments, it's awkward being the solo single mom of the entire beaming, glowing pregnant crowd. It's moments like these you appreciate your family by your side and loving you through the most difficult challenges.

I often find myself hiding my ring finger now that I'm pregnant. When a stranger or someone from my distant past asks me when my baby is due, because they see my big belly, I notice that I hide my left hand. I do it without even thinking about it. My shame causes the natural reaction of my left hand moving behind my back. I like to be proud and feel strong no matter where I'm at in life, but I subconsciously feel vulnerable to the judgment of others.

When I first started doing my job searches after returning to the United States, I considered buying a ring to wear on my ring finger so that people wouldn't judge me. I hate that I hide my finger. It's almost like I can't help it.

I'm on my daily walk, trying to keep some stamina in this slowing and tired body of mine. I pass a garage sale and see baby clothes, bottles, and other items. I walk over and look around, thinking I may find something for my baby girl.

The woman hosting the garage sale starts chatting with me about my pregnancy. She has a daughter who is now older, maybe seven or eight years old.

We start comparing stories on our pregnancies and realize I'm in the middle of a journey similar to one she's already been on. She tells me that she was fired from her job as a waitress when she got pregnant. Her boyfriend left her as well. She had to move back in with her parents to make it through that season of her life. Although difficult, she said losing her job turned out to be a great blessing because of the time she was able to spend with her new baby. It saddened her that the dad missed out on all the precious moments during her pregnancy and early baby years. She describes how joyful it was to wake up in the morning and lie in bed with her baby girl, breastfeeding her and listening to her happy coos.

She tells me another story about a grocery-shopping experience. One day, at the store, an elderly woman began scolding her because she was not wearing a wedding ring and therefore was pregnant and unwed. She ended up buying herself a ring to wear because she didn't want the extra pressure from others about her marital status. She, like me, had intentions of having a lasting relationship with the man who she conceived with even prior to pregnancy, and was rejected.

She and her daughter's father eventually got back together and are now married. She's really happy but admitted it was difficult to reconcile the relationship after the painful rejection.

We enjoy sharing our stories and she's curious to see how things turn out for me.

"Things work out for a reason," she says.

Although I've heard this statement more times at this juncture in my life than ever before, I always enjoy hearing it again.

In hopes of returning to my job as a firefighter, I've been taking classes to avoid a hiatus in my training. I'm seven months pregnant, donning my bunker pants, and about to participate in my fire-rescue class. We're going to cut up cars today. My belly is protruding over my bunker pants as I pull the straps up onto my shoulders and place my jacket over my arms.

A couple of old cars have been donated to the program for firefighters to practice rescue scenarios. Practice consists of vehicle stabilization, cutting off and bending doors, peeling back the steering wheel, breaking and cutting out all the windows, and more.

This class is full of younger kids who are seeking a career in fire or EMS. Most of them have started to volunteer at the local fire department and are eager to learn. I'm one of the few older students, but I've enjoyed the presence of youthful firefighters with unjaded spirits. They're excited for me to pick up the Jaws of Life and show them how a pregnant firefighter does work. I'm a little hesitant because I know my strength and balance aren't the best right now.

"Come on, Lizzy, take a turn. You can do it!"

I pick up the Jaws of Life and cautiously prepare to cut the hinges of the car door. With my gloves and other personal protective equipment on, I make a few cuts through the door and help pull it away from the vehicle. That's about all I can handle right now in my condition, but I feel excited to participate in fire training.

Soon I will find out if this is something I will get to do for the rest of my life, or not.

I've communicated as much as I could and tried to get the okay to return to my job. This is an awkward scenario because I realize this is a physical job and I know that I cannot be a firefighter in the literal sense until after I have my daughter. There are numerous nonphysical jobs all around the firehouse that are performed every day, and demanding calls are not all that common on a regular basis. Surely, there's something I can do in the meantime.

I realize this is an abnormal situation and I can completely understand why I wouldn't get my job back. I know there are many departments that understand this natural occurrence and are familiar with accommodating females to continue work without losing their jobs. In the meantime, I tried everything I could to contribute. I was bringing back almost a whole new me, a more confident, more cultured, more trained me. I knew I was an asset before I went overseas, and I believe that was the case even more so now, especially now that I'm pregnant. I've run numerous calls dealing with pregnancies, miscarriages, and bleeding. I understand those parts of life a lot more now and would be an excellent caregiver for those female patients.

Imagine being eight months pregnant and walking in to say you want your job back as a firefighter.

I knew I would be rejected, but I had to put my fear aside and follow through with this incredibly uncomfortable situation. There is much to do besides fight fires at this station, and I wanted a chance.

In the end, I received the answer, and it wasn't what I had hoped for. I was told there was nothing I could contribute in my condition and I couldn't be reinstated.

This was heart wrenching, although somewhat predictable. Had I quit pushing forward and quit trying because of intimidation, I could never have been satisfied with myself. I would've always wondered how things would've been if I had given up.

The door to that part of my life is shut—not just shut but slammed shut. Leaving behind the culture and lifestyle of a firefighter is incredibly difficult. I will probably always feel like a firefighter at heart.

Chapter 22

The Birth

MY DUE DATE HAS COME and gone—still no baby. Each night, I wonder if my water will break, and I wake up disappointed. Sleeping has been uncomfortable. My big belly is in the way and I can't relax. I'm used to sleeping on my stomach, or my back, but now I can only sleep on my side. I feel so big!

I sit in the doctor's office, half-naked except for the blue and white smock. I'm still not used to getting these exams, though I've had several. I'm hopeful that my cervix is dilated or at least something to show my baby girl is coming soon.

The doctor examines me, and there are no signs of my pending labor. "Well, we don't want the baby to be too overdue because it can stress the baby. We can induce you as soon as tonight (which is a Wednesday), or you can come in on Sunday. I'm off Thursday through Saturday."

I'm nervous but filled with excitement at the idea. But now I'm also a little confused because I don't want to choose my baby's due date. This feels like too big of a responsibility. I tell her I'll wait on my decision and then I'll call the office.

My dad and I go out for my favorite pregnancy breakfast of Egg McMuffin while I make my decision.

"I just want her to come on God's time," I say. "I feel weird about picking her birth date."

Right after I express that thought, another thought quickly follows. "I suppose we use doctors and medicine to keep people from dying so I guess it's similar but on the opposite spectrum."

"Well ..." I pondered again. "I suppose God created wisdom and gave us the ability to do all these things."

As you can tell, I'm really rationalizing this whole concept, to make things feel right in my own mind. Okay, I'm really overthinking this whole thing, and maybe being a little silly. Main point: I just want my baby to come out already. I can't wait to meet her, and my body hurts!

I call my doctor and tell her I will come in this evening to start the process of induction.

My mom and I arrive to the hospital at 7:30 p.m. and we're shown into the birthing room. I walk in with a diaper bag on my shoulder filled with baby's first outfits and a blanky. The woman gives us a quick tour of the room and shows me the Jacuzzi tub in my bathroom.

I look at the narrow bed and ask if I should go ahead and sit on it. I'm not used to seeing patients just walk in and sit on the hospital bed, so it seems strange. Normally, people are rolled in on gurneys and transferred to the hospital bed. The nurse has me change into a hospital gown and then gives me an Ambien so I'm able to rest.

Right away, they begin a regimen of tablet insertions into my vagina to thin the cervix. The tablets will be inserted every few hours throughout the night, which is why the sleep aid is necessary to help me rest with the occasional interruptions.

At 7:30 a.m. I'm served hospital food. I will start the Pitocin drip to induce contractions at 9:00 a.m., and I will no longer be able to eat any food at that point.

I fill up the Jacuzzi tub and turn on the jets. The bath is even more relaxing than I anticipated. I don't want to get out. I lean back and relax, and then I dip my head under the water. One of the jets hits the back of my hair and I feel it instantly gnarl and tangle in the force of the pressurized water, but it's too late to react. I come up for air and put my hand behind my head. The strong jets create a tight tangle in my hair. I quickly grab the conditioner and pile it into my scraggly hair to see if I can work out the knots. This reminds me of firefighting and how knotted my hair got after structure fires and long drills. My bunker jacket constantly rubbed knots into my fine hair. I spent a lot of time removing dreadlocks in that occupation.

All right, no more Jacuzzi time. I put on a clean hospital nightgown to get ready for my big day. It's time to get serious. Time to have a baby!

I walk over to my bed and feel a warm liquid dripping down my legs. I look down in confusion. The nurse is standing by.

"Is that—? Did my water just break?" I ask the nurse.

"Yep! Sure looks like it," she replies with a smile.

"Sorry," I say to her about the mess I just made on the floor, even though I know I couldn't help it.

"It's not a problem," she says while cleaning it up.

I lie down on the bed, not knowing what to expect at this time. Gradually, I begin to feel pain in my lower back and abdomen.

My mom asks me what she can do to help.

"I don't know," I reply.

As my contractions start to get stronger, the nurse shows my mom how she can rub my lower back aggressively during the painful phase.

The contractions keep coming, and they get stronger and more painful. Burning, squeezing pains shoot through me. Every time, my mom rubs my lower back in an aggressive circular motion.

The nurse asks if I want some medicine for comfort.

"Not yet," I reply in a pathetic voice.

Almost two hours pass and I'm still having contractions. I finally give in to an injection of pain relief.

Now everything around me suddenly appears brightly colored like a circus full of clowns. I feel drugged out of my mind.

I turn to my mom and ask, "Did the nurse just come in and talk to me?"

"Yes, she did."

I can't tell reality from this weird circus dream. And I can still feel all the pain from the contractions. The thing is I just don't remember them after they happen because this medicine makes me feel so brain dead.

The medicine starts to wear off and the nurse asks me if I want more. I must've said yes because the crazy circus comes back to confuse me.

A little while later, my brain feels fuzzy, but I'm finally sober enough to tell the nurse I'm ready for the epidural.

Another nurse comes in and has me sit up in bed while a needle is strategically placed into my spine. My pelvis goes numb, as does my right leg.

Now I'm finally out of the crazy circus and can hardly recall what just happened with the last few hours of my life. My mind is clear and I sit up to visit with my family. The monitor shows that I'm still having contractions, but I can't feel them at all.

I look down at my white legs that are swollen from weight gain and fluid buildup. My right leg has started to drift off the bed, but I hadn't noticed because it's completely numb. I have to grab the leg with both hands and physically position it back onto the center of the bed. I poke at the numb limb, unable to feel anything.

The day goes by quickly and nurses come in to check on the status of my cervix.

I only dilate a few centimeters and there's no progress for hours. The doctor is starting to consider giving me a C-section. I tell her I want to do everything I can to avoid a C-section.

It's 9:00 p.m. and the nurses can't tell if my cervix is fully dilated. They've mentioned throughout the day that my cervix is difficult to find. One lady inserts her finger to locate my cervix and thinks I may be fully dilated, but she can't tell. She sends in another nurse and confirms that it's time to start delivery.

"I'll call in the doctor," she says.

No other expectant moms are in the birthing unit. It's empty and quiet upstairs. It's dark outside and the curtains of my hospital window are open. I can see the stars twinkling in the dark.

The doctor has one nurse hold my foot and my mom holds my other foot. Normally, this would seem very awkward, but when you're pregnant and about to have a baby, all modesty goes out the window. I'm not really worried about being exposed; this is just how it goes.

I'm sleepy after such a physical demand has been placed on my body today. The doctor tells me I will push as hard as I can during the contractions. Since I have the epidural in, I can't feel my contractions. She will watch the monitor and tell me when to push and for how long.

"Push!" she says.

I hold my breath and bear down as hard as I can until she tells me to relax.

"Good job, Lizzy," she encourages.

"Ready, and push!"

The doctor keeps encouraging me and I find myself actually feeling strong while I push. For all I know, I'm pushing the same as any other mom in labor, but this doctor is making me feel like a champion. I feel good; I feel strong. I have no pain and the epidural is doing its job.

I keep thinking my baby will be out any time, but I look at the clock and see that an hour has passed. It's almost tomorrow. Maybe my baby won't be born today.

I keep pushing with all my might. I'm so exhausted and the hospital is so peaceful right now. All this pushing is giving me the same chemical release as a hard workout. I feel the endorphins releasing. In-between pushes, I fall asleep because I'm so relaxed.

"Push!" the doctor says as she wakes me from my short naps.

Finally, it's after 11:00 p.m. and I've started to crown. My baby's head is coming out.

"Wow! Look at that full head of hair," the nurse says. "You should feel it!"

I put my hand down between my legs and the nurse helps me to gently touch my daughters head. I feel thick, wet, curly hair on top of her little head, and my hand pulls back quickly because of the unexpected texture.

Just the top of her head is out and now I have to push hard to complete the birthing process. I push with every ounce of force that

I have within me. I push and I push until the doctor pulls her out and I can see my baby's beautiful body as she starts to cry.

They clean Yasmine up and place her in my arms. Finally, I can embrace my precious new daughter. The nurse tells me that mother and baby will bond better skin to skin. She said I should take my shirt off and let my daughter lie on my chest with just her diaper on.

The nurses help me to feed her so she will stop crying. Afterward, my daughter falls asleep cuddled on my chest and I am beyond happy with this little precious being that I've been carrying around for the last nine months. I can hardly believe this is real. She's in my arms and she's so amazing. My heart is filled with love.

Chapter 23

The Visitation

Dear Yasmine,

You are two months old now, and your daddy came and met you this week. He was so excited to finally get to meet you and hold you. He's been calling me most days and asking me how you are doing. I've been giving him day-by-day updates on your quick growth from all the tummy pains and pukey times to your happy moments and smiles. He flew from Baghdad to Dubai to San Antonio to Portland just to hold you for a few days. He also brought along his mom, your abuelita, to meet you.

A LEX AND I STARTED SHARING better communication as my date to give birth arose. My anger toward him long subsided because I had lost all feelings for him. I noticed that the more we communicated, I could sense his excitement and loyalty toward our unborn baby. During our first conversations of the pregnancy, we weren't quite ready to talk about our pending parental partnership, so we would cut the awkwardness by talking about firefighting, Iraq, and the mutual friends that we had met and lived with while overseas.

After many months of having no interest in Alex, I slowly began to remember the reasons why I liked him so much in the first place and grew apprehensive as to what our future would look like. My emotions ran between excitement and fear of him meeting his daughter. Would he love her? Would he treat me well? Would he try to get involved with me again? I had so many questions and concerns running through my mind.

I decided I was excited for him to visit, but I will never be in a relationship with him again because of how things turned out.

I'm also angry because I feel so deprived of a man's love. Every new mom deserves to be nurtured, and I crave that affection right now. I need to know that I'm loved and cared for. I feel like he took that away from me. No man has ever made me feel so unattractive, so unimpressive, and so unimportant in my whole life. That was a major shock to my self-esteem. I fear I'll be permanently affected by what I perceive as his perspective of me. How will I ever feel sexy and confident with another man without remembering how worthless I was to someone else? I just can't let myself think like that. I need to think positive.

Alex booked a hotel in Portland for the four of us to stay at. I told him that we could share a room so that he could help me at night and get up with our daughter to feed her. The only caveat was that the room would have to have two beds. I was proud for setting that precedence straight with him.

Alex and his mother arrived at the airport and Yasmine and I picked them up and drove to the hotel. Alex and I got along naturally and talked to one another comfortably, as if we were good friends. His mom was so sweet, as I suspected. She and I spoke on the phone a few times before, because she wanted to connect with me and her new grandbaby. She speaks much more English than I do Spanish, but we still had some difficulties communicating with our language and accent barrier.

During the time we stayed together, he continuously impressed me with his actions. He obviously loved and admired our daughter very much, and he was thoughtful and kind to me as well. At a restaurant, when our daughter was crying and I had to hold her, he fed me. He paid for all accommodations and even brushed the hair away from my eyes while participating in pseudo-family portraits. Things could not have gone any more pleasant.

I was also very pleased that regardless of the desires that did arise, we were not intimate the whole time. We did, however, hold each other cautiously, but caringly for some moments. With his arms around me and Yasmine, I felt a feeling I'd never felt before, the feeling of having my own complete family. It was one of the greatest feelings I've ever had.

Chapter 24

The Fires of Life

WHEN GOLD IS PUT UNDER extreme heat, it turns from a solid to a liquid. The imperfections from within the gold will rise to the top as a black residue. That residue can then be removed, improving the quality of the gold, or it can be hardened back into a solid, allowing the imperfections to stay within. Think about that.

Just as fire burns out the imperfections of gold, the trials of life bring forward the imperfections in our life giving us an opportunity to see the ways we can change. The "fires" in our life can allow us an opportunity to acknowledge ways in which we need to change. Trust that God will take you through the fire to success and you will be better because of it. "Count it all joy when you fall into various trials, knowing that the testing of your faith produces patience" (James 1:2-3).

Since God knows the beginning, the middle, and the end of our lives, He knew my weaknesses and foresaw the poor choices I would make as well as the positive choices. God can make miracles out of mistakes and poor choices because He gives grace. I've felt myself walking through the metaphorical fires of life. As I've passed through the trials, I've grown closer to God. I'm now trying to follow the path that He wants me on, and listening for His still, small voice.

I reminisce on all the fun and positive times as a firefighter, times of hard work and camaraderie. I miss running calls, throwing on my bunker gear, and feeling the strength of the fire engine through the accelerator under my foot. I miss the various complexities of calls requiring innovation and forethought as well as the quiet moments of comforting someone who is truly sick.

Now I'm on a new journey. I see life through a renewed spirit and a stronger faith. I have a beautiful daughter who I am madly in love with, and I know this is God's plan for me.

Life has been good and challenging as a single mom. I'm patiently waiting to see what my future holds while pursuing my goals along the way. I've grown closer to my family as they've opened up their homes to me during this transitional season of my life.

Alex has been great, and it's been fun communicating with him on Skype. His face lights up when he sees our daughter.

"She's getting so big!" he says frequently as she crawls around in her little diapered bottom.

I find myself very enamored by his kindness and care toward me and Yasmine. *Do I have a crush on him?* I wonder. I don't think he feels the same for me though, and I'm so fearful of putting myself into a vulnerable position.

I stare off into the countryside, contemplating my future, while bundled up in a blanket on the porch swing. I wrap my palms around a mug of coffee, hoping to borrow some of its warmth.

The sun is peeking up above the mountains and I'm surrounded by the serene beauty of the countryside. I see a field of tall wheat grass swaying gently in the breeze.

I take a drink of my morning coffee that is steaming against the cool morning air.

Well, maybe I will never find love again, I conclude as the humbling thought comes to me on this peaceful morning. I've prayed that God will guide me to a good man if it's in His will to do so. Now I can just sit back and see what He has in store for me. It's nice to no longer worry about these things when I can just put them in His hands.

"Thank You, God," I find myself saying as I smile lightly. I feel confident that I can be happy and satisfied whether I am with or without a man by my side. Even if it's ten or more years from now, when I do meet the man that I will love, I know I will be okay.

I finally feel fulfilled with just myself and the big man upstairs. How funny! I used to think it was so strange if someone spoke as if they knew and loved God personally. Now here I am, loving God so much, feeling complete confidence and fulfillment in my relationship with only Him. Surely I will now be the misunderstood one who talks about loving God. I guess once you know Him, it no longer matters if it seems strange to others. I finally have found the piece of my life that was missing—the fulfillment to my constant emptiness. I've filled the "God-shaped space" in my heart that could only be filled by His presence in my life.

I feel like I can finally breathe some relief for the first time in years. I followed my own path for so long and made so many poor choices until I felt aged and weary. I felt dried out, hardened, and sober. I finally told God, "Okay God, please take my life into Your hands. Help me to hear You, because I can't do this without You."

The challenges surrounding me became greater in negativity. I couldn't always understand what His plan was, but I continued to put my trust in Him and hold onto faith.

The facade of my life may seem unimpressive and cause others to pass judgment. I'm a twenty-nine-year-old single mom living with my parents. But what they don't see is that the foundation of my life is stronger. I'm no longer trying to build my life from the outside in. I'm stronger inside and building the foundation of my life from the inside out. This is just the beginning, and I'm so excited to see where things will go from here. I'm thankful for the simple things and constantly assessing where I need to grow.

If this story were a movie, this ending may seem anticlimactic to some, but not to me. I'm learning to find peace amid the storms, find good in the difficult times, to forgive myself as well as others, to not define myself or others by our past choices. I'm seeing that God can soften even the hardest of hearts and change the way we treat others. I'm learning to live off wisdom and guidance instead of the whim of emotions. Enjoying every season of life, no matter what, if it's where I want to be or not. If this were the end of the story, I would be perfectly content right here in this moment—*if* this were the end of the story.

Ten months after Alex's first visit with his daughter, he was able to come home from Iraq again to see his beautiful baby girl. He anticipated this reunion for a long time, hoping it would be sooner, but there were issues with entrance and exit visas.

We finally reunite in time for Yasmine's first birthday.

I've grown fond of Alex throughout our many online conversations and Skyping. It's clear how proud he is of his baby girl. We laugh together at her adorable ways as she crawls around and babbles in her own language.

I encourage their relationship and point at him on the screen, saying, "Hi, Daddy!"

I struggle lightly with the idea of the unknown. Who will Alex marry someday and bring into my daughter's life? I want her to have a great relationship with her daddy, but what's this going to be like? It's going to get expensive for plane tickets to fly between states for visitations. I try not to focus on the fear and negativity, and I emphasize the positive points. The truth is, her dad and I are getting along very well. We're developing a trust and a friendship through our communications. Pride and hurt feelings are pushed aside for a greater cause: the happiness of our daughter.

After six hours of travel, Yasmine and I arrive in Texas, the same state I met Alex just two years ago. It seems like so much longer than two years. Alex and I exchange a quick hug and I hand Yasmine over so he can hold her.

A couple of days into our stay, we begin to feel that feeling again with the three of us together, the feeling that we are a family. Alex flirts with me and shows me bits of unexpected affection. Even with this flirtation, I have no expectations; I don't see him ever wanting to be with me. I decide to just enjoy the company and stay strong. I don't want to be hurt again.

I'm seeing a whole new side of Alex. I wasn't sure if he was just on good behavior back in Portland, but he really is a very patient and kindhearted man. Even while driving in traffic he is calm, when I would probably be hollering at the car in front of me. He puts me to shame with his calm presence, and I find myself wanting to be a little more patient by his example. I also see a light in his eyes that was missing before. In a strange way, it almost looks like his soul has returned to him. He no longer appears to be an empty shell.

I created a different image of Alex in my mind. Although I don't like the choices he made in our situation, I'm humbled by my own past. I think we've all done things in our past that we realize later we would never do again. How could I condemn him and define him by this one instance, when I don't want to be defined by my own past choices. How would that be right? Still, I don't want to be hasty and make myself vulnerable to a repeat of history. He seems like a very good man and maybe it wouldn't be so wrong to consider him to be a part of my life again.

A couple more days pass and I feel the divide between us shrinking. I feel myself falling for him, and I'm seeing an admiration in his eyes toward me that I've never seen.

Our daughter is now one year old and we celebrate with a big birthday bash. Decorations are everywhere and the piñata is ready for bashing. Pictures are taken of the three of us together and I love it, but I feel a little awkward because I don't want to be too expectant. Alex comforts me with a caring hug from behind, and I feel my heart melt.

I never thought I would ever be in a relationship with this man again, but here we are together flirting, embracing one another, and kissing again. We're actually falling in love. I never saw it coming.

A year later, Yasmine and I move to Texas to be with Alex. He leaves his job in Iraq to come home to us for good. Yasmine loves her daddy as if he's been here all along. And the exciting news is, he wants to marry me. I have a shiny ring on my finger to prove it.

Not in my wildest dreams did I see any of this coming. I have an amazing fiancée, a beautiful daughter, and I'm living halfway across the country just feeling blessed and thankful for the adventures I've had.

I am deeply and passionately in love with Alex. He is my very best friend, and just having him by my side brightens every nuance of an ordinary day. And our daughter is amazing, of course. Her smile melts my heart, and I just can't get enough of her.

It brings tears to my eyes when I look over at Alex by my side with our daughter. She has her mommy and daddy together and she's so happy. We almost lost this family. The fact that we are all together is purely by the good grace and blessings of God. I sit in awe and amazement of His grace.

Epilogue

I CAN VIVIDLY RECALL A still and quiet night when I was eight years old. It was a night that I was up later than my parents, so all the comfortable ambient sounds had quieted, leaving a young child to feel vulnerable, as if being awake later than my family would put me in some sort of danger. Regardless of nighttime fears, my mind was full of inspiration, and I was feeling ambitious. I pulled out a spiral notebook and a pencil. I ripped the lined paper from the spiral binding, leaving a tattered edge of multiple, tiny, ripped holes as it pulled away. I then began to write a book. I wasn't searching for ideas to write a fictional story; I wanted to write something about my life. As an average second grader, I didn't have anything special to tell, so I'm still not sure why I was inspired.

I started out the story saying something about my dad traveling as a merchant marine, and after about two sentences, I couldn't think of anything else to write. I then drew a horrible self-portrait, novel-cover-size, of course, and put it on top of the page where I began my first memoir.

For a few years, I kept that strange self-portrait of my full disproportioned body from the side profile. I finally tossed it away out of embarrassment that someone may find it. But I've always had a small inkling of desire to continue some sort of a story. Although I was a horrible writer in school and couldn't see how I could possibly write a whole book I knew that there would be a day I would write one.

God has a story of victory for everyone's life, if we are willing to just follow Him. What is yours?